LITTLE G

CLASSIC
SONGS

LITTLE GIANT® ENCYCLOPEDIA

CLASSIC SONGS

EDITED BY MATTHEW BARTON
WITH AN INTRODUCTION BY B.J. THOMAS

STERLING

New York / London
www.sterlingpublishing.com

STERLING and the distinctive Sterling logo are registered trademarks of
Sterling Publishing Co., Inc.

Library of Congress Cataloging-in-Publication Data
Little giant encyclopedia of classic songs / edited by Matthew Barton.
p. cm.
Includes index.
ISBN-13: 978-1-4027-5638-2
ISBN-10: 1-4027-5638-0
1. Songs, English—Texts. 2. Folk songs, English—Texts. I. Barton,
Matthew.

ML54.6.L445 2008
782.42'0268—dc22

2007032215

2 4 6 8 10 9 7 5 3 1

Published by Sterling Publishing Co., Inc.
387 Park Avenue South, New York, NY 10016

© 2008 by Sterling Publishing Co., Inc.

Distributed in Canada by Sterling Publishing
^{c}/o Canadian Manda Group, 165 Dufferin Street
Toronto, Ontario, Canada M6K 3H6
Distributed in the United Kingdom by GMC Distribution Services
Castle Place, 166 High Street, Lewes, East Sussex, England BN7 1XU
Distributed in Australia by Capricorn Link (Australia) Pty. Ltd.
P.O. Box 704, Windsor, NSW 2756, Australia

Printed in China
All rights reserved

Sterling ISBN-13: 978-1-4027-5638-2
ISBN-10: 1-4027-5638-0

Designed by Monica Gurevich

For information about custom editions, special sales, premium and
corporate purchases, please contact Sterling Special Sales
Department at 800-805-5489 or specialsales@sterlingpublishing.com

TABLE OF CONTENTS

FOREWORD

❧ FOREWORD ❧

Songs come in all shapes and sizes. Although this book is called an encyclopedia of song, it can't provide the last word on singing—no book or song can.

But we've tried to provide you with some of the best lyrics that people still love to sing. Some are still being sung hundreds of years after they were written, and most of them probably have at least a few hundred more years of life left in them. No matter how old it is, a song lives when somebody sings it—so live it up!

The authors of many songs are unknown to us, and it's likely that such songs actually had many authors who shaped and edited the words and music until they were sure to stand the test of time. Nowadays, a song is just as likely to circulate in a file attachment as it is in a book such as this, but songs and singers still need each other the way they always have.

The known authors in this book include Stephen Foster, who gets a chapter of his own, as well as a wordsmiths from Robert Burns to Irving Berlin. The styles range from ballads to blues. Their roots are everywhere from Merrie Olde England to Tin Pan Alley.

Some songs are strictly from the authors' imaginations, while others are straight out of history. Some are about love. Some are about war. Some are for work, hard work, but just as many are strictly for play. All are for singing! We've tried to maintain the authentic spellings so that they can be sung the way they were intended. Enjoy!

INTRODUCTION

❧ INTRODUCTION ❧

As you look through the pages of this encyclopedia of classic songs, you will, time and again, hear music playing somewhere in your mind. A faint voice from a distant part of your past will sing the lyrics to you as you read them. With some of these fine songs, you will recall that you heard them at a religious service, on the radio, or at a concert. Others will bring to mind a cherished Christmas memory or a favorite movie or musical. Still others will come back to you with their haunting melody without revealing their origins and how you became acquainted with them.

I believe this experience will surely happen to you because the songs in this book are part of the American psyche. Before I even knew that music was something that I really wanted to do, many of these songs were there with me as part of my own identity and spiritual being. As I have traveled back and forth across our great country many times performing music for folks, the spirit of these songs has been ever present. What the *Little Giant®* *Encyclopedia: Classic Songs* provides are the actual, correct lyrics of many popular songs and also the lesser known second and later verses that are just as beautiful.

"Amazing Grace," "Rock-a-Bye Baby," and "Take Me Out to the Ball Game" are at the core of the American experience (even though one of them was written as a hymn by an Englishman). It's not as if when children are young they seek these songs out to learn them. It is almost like they are scrubbed into the pores from the bath water. Of course, hardly anyone is familiar with the verses to the song that we use to celebrate baseball, but here they are for you.

True to the American experience, with people from all over the world coming here to settle and make a life, the songs from their native lands came with their trunks, baggage and memories of the old country. "Danny Boy," "My Bonny Lies Over the Ocean," and "Auld Lang Syne" are three such memorable songs.

About twenty years ago I was performing a show on New Year's Eve. Just before the announcer called me to the stage, the promoter told me I had to sing "Auld Lang Syne." The news hit me hard as I had never played the song in concert or in rehearsal. I was worried that I didn't know the song well enough as I hadn't practiced it or even looked at the lyrics. There was no time to do a quick run through or get the words. The only thing the promoter said when I expressed my concern was, "You'll do fine."

And you know what? He was right. As the music swelled and the countdown to a new year ended in cheers, the band picked up the tune like it was right there in their back pocket. I found myself remembering Robert Burn's famous old poem from all those times of hearing Guy Lombardo and his band play it. I jumped into that memory and belted it out. We didn't miss a beat.

As you look at the Christmas songs, you will see that they cover the full gamut of what the holiday encompasses. The songs not only interpret the narrative of the birth of Jesus from different perspectives, but also include the traditions and customs from many European cultures that have become part of the modern Christmas experience. And don't forget Santa Claus and his reindeer. "Silent Night" is such a beautiful song. It is not that complicated in its structure. In many ways, the melody is derivative of a quaint lullaby. Many entertainers have recorded "Silent Night" because of its simple beauty and how much depth of feeling can be instilled in the lyrics.

In times of national crisis or doubt, the collective conscious of the country looks back to the great songs of old. Songs that recall happier times and the patriotic songs that bring forth our courage and pride are remembered and sang. "You're a Grand Old Flag," "America the

Beautiful," "The Battle Cry of Freedom" and even "It's a Long Way to Tipperary" return to help us through the dark times.

As this book clearly illustrates, *Love,* as a topic for a song, never goes out of style. When I was just a little boy, I used to sing a sweet little tune to my mom called "I Want a Girl."

The full line in the song that she loved was, "I want a girl just like the girl that married dear old Dad," meaning I wanted a girl just a nice and pretty as my mother. I am happy to tell you that I did find that girl in my bride of close to 40 years. That song and the wonderful feelings and memories it captured left an indelible mark on me. So much so that I am sure parts of that song spawned other songs for me. I took those feelings and created a more updated version for the modern listener without ever really being aware I was doing it. The idea was probably lying there in wait for many years until an event or memory triggered the music to play just as I was looking for inspiration for a new song.

As far as the Blues go, you have got to spend a little time in your skin before you can really understand what the Blues is all about. When I was little, about 12 or 13 years old, I used to sneak out of the house at night and head down to the local blues shack in Houston. I really had this thing for Bobby "Blue" Bland and his band. I just could not help myself and braved the dangers of wandering the streets late at night to see these guys jam. Man, they were smoking hot. Bobby would tease me, calling me Elvis, but he would watch out for me because he knew I was just a kid. Though he was from Memphis, when I would find out he was playing in Houston, I just had to find a way to get out. Maybe I just knew I was seeing something special, as he's now in the Rock and Roll Hall of Fame and he's still out there singing the blues. I also looked up to guys like Fats Domino, B.B. King, and Chuck Berry.

Before I end, I must give a tip of my cap to Stephen Foster and his amazing body of work. When he got into his groove he really nailed it. It seems to me that Bob Dylan picked up where Foster left off with his prolific career.

As you look at this book, you may not immediately remember all the melodies of these tunes. But once you hear it again or remember it, the song will take you back to a time or a place in your life, or more often than not, to a great old memory. I've traveled all over the world playing music and it is good American music that people everywhere love. Maybe you can identify with how these classic songs have touched my life and influenced my career. I hope that as you peruse them, you will let the music lead you to your own fond memories.

—B.J. Thomas

CHAPTER

1

Favorite Irish Songs

HERE'S a sampling of Irish songs, both humorous and sentimental. Many of the songs that later generations have found to be quintessentially Irish originated not on Irish soil but on New York City's Tin Pan Alley, the legendary lane of song given its name by the constant day and night clattering of hit-hungry tunesmiths and their typewriters. In the late nineteenth and early twentieth centuries they supplied a ready market of first-, second-, and third-generation Irish-Americans with songs that extolled Ireland's beauty and saluted its American sons and daughters.

It didn't take long for a good song to pass into legend. Long before *Riverdance*, stage shows were celebrating Ireland's beauty and its mythic past. James Royce Shannon, for instance, wrote "Too-ra-loo-ra-loo-ral" (page 26) for an Irish-themed Broadway show in 1913. By the time that Bing Crosby sang it for Barry Fitzgerald in the 1944 film classic *Going My Way*, it seemed as though everyone's Irish "mither" had sung it to them as they rocked in their cradle beneath a thatched roof in the Emerald Isle.

In Ireland itself, the standard in popular poetry and song was set by Thomas Moore (1779-1852). He excelled at sentimental and romantic lyrics, but also celebrated heroic and patriotic themes in an era when Ireland was still ruled by England. He praised tragic heroes like "The Minstrel-Boy" (page 37) and the beauties of "Believe me/If All Those Endearing Young Charms" (page 33) with equal skill.

Danny Boy

By Frederick Weatherly

Oh Danny Boy, the pipes, the pipes are calling,
From glen to glen, and down the mountain side,
The summer's gone, and all the flowers are dying,
'Tis you, 'tis you must go and I must bide.

But come ye back when summer's in the meadow,
Or when the valley's hushed and white with snow,
'Tis I'll be there in sunshine or in shadow,
Oh Danny Boy, oh Danny Boy, I love you so.

And when you come, when all the flowers are dying,
And I am dead, as dead I well may be,
You'll come and find the place where I am lying,
And kneel and say an "Avé" there for me.

And I shall hear, tho' soft you tread above me,
And all my dreams shall warm and sweeter be,
If you'll not fail to tell me that you love me,
I'll simply sleep in peace until you come to me.

Harrigan

By George M. Cohan

Who is the man who will spend or will even lend?
Harrigan, That's Me!
Who is your friend when you find that you,
Need a friend?
Harrigan, That's Me!
For I'm just as proud of my name you see,
As an Emperor, Czar or a King, could be,
Who is the man helps a man every time he can?
Harrigan, That's Me!

❀

Chorus:
H -A - double R - I - G - A - N spells Harrigan,
Proud of all the Irish blood that's in me,
Divil a man can say a word agin' me,
H - A - double R - I - G - A - N, you see,
Is a name that a shame never has been connected with,
Harrigan, That's me!

❀

Who is the man never stood for a gad about?
Harrigan, That's Me!
Who is the man that the town's simply mad about?

Harrigan, That's Me!
The ladies and babies are fond of me,
I'm fond of them, too, in return, you see,
Who is the gent that's deserving a monument?
Harrigan, That's Me!

❀

Chorus

I'll Take You Home Again Kathleen

By Thomas Westendorf

I'll take you home again, Kathleen,
Across the ocean wild and wide,
To where your heart has ever been,
Since you were first my bonnie bride,
The roses all have left your cheek,
I've watched them fade away and die,
Your voice is sad when ever you speak,
And tears bedim your loving eyes.

🌸

Chorus:
Oh! I will take you back, Kathleen,
To where your heart will feel no pain,
And when the fields are fresh and green,
I'll take you to your home again!

🌸

I know you love me, Kathleen, dear,
Your heart was ever fond and true,
I always feel when you are near,
That life holds nothing, dear, but you,
The smiles that once you gave to me,

I scarcely ever see them now,
Though many, many times I see,
A dark'ning shadow on your brow.

🌼

Chorus

🌼

To that dear home beyond the sea,
My Kathleen shall again return,
And when thy old friends welcome thee,
Thy loving heart will cease to yearn,
Where laughs the little silver stream,
Beside your mother's humble cot,
And brightest rays of sunshine gleam,
There all your grief will be forgot.

🌼

Chorus

Peg O' My Heart

Oh! My heart's in a whirl over one little girl,
I love her, I love her, yes, I do,
Altho' her heart is far away,
I hope to make her mine some day,
Ev'ry beautiful rose, ev'ry violet knows,
I love her, I love her fond and true,
And her heart fondly sighs, as I sing to her eyes,
Her eyes of blue,
Sweet eyes of blue, my darling!

Peg O' My Heart, I love you,
We'll never part, I love you,
Dear little girl, sweet little girl,
Sweeter than the rose of Erin,
Are your winning smiles endearin',
Peg O' My Heart, your glances,
With Irish art entrance me,
Come, be my own, come, make your home in my heart.

When your heart's full of fears,
And your eyes full of tears,
I'll kiss them, I'll kiss them all away,
For, like the gold that's in your hair,

Is all the love for you I bear,
O, believe in me, do,
I'm as lonesome as you,
I miss you, I miss you all the day,
Let the light of live shine from your eyes into mine,
And shine for aye,
Sweetheart for aye, my darling!

Too-ra-loo-ra-loo-ral

By James Royce Shannon

Over in Killarney,
Many years ago,
Me mither sang a song to me,
In tones so sweet and low,
Just a simple little ditty,
In her good ould Irish way,
And I'd give the world if she could sing,
That song to me this day.

Chorus:
Too-ra-loo-ra-loo-ral,
Too-ra-loo-ra-li,
Too-ra-loo-ra-loo-ral,
Hush, now don't you cry!
Too-ra-loo-ra-loo-ral,
Too-ra-loo-ra-li,
Too-ra-loo-ra-loo-ral,
That's an Irish lullaby.

Oft, in dreams I wander,
To that cot again,
I feel her arms a huggin' me,

As when she held me then,
And I hear her voice a hummin',
To me as in days of yore,
When she used to rock me fast asleep,
Outside the cabin door.

❦

Chorus

When Irish Eyes are Smiling

By Chauncey Olcott, George Graff, Jr., and Ernest Ball

There's a tear in your eye,
And I'm wondering why,
For it never should be there at all,
With such pow'r in your smile,
Sure a stone you'd beguile,
So there's never a teardrop should fall,
When your sweet lilting laughter's,
Like some fairy song,
And your eyes twinkle bright as can be,
You should laugh all the while,
And all other times smile,
And now, smile a smile for me.

Chorus:
When Irish eyes are smiling,
Sure, 'tis like the morn in Spring,
In the lilt of Irish laughter,
You can hear the angels sing,
When Irish hearts are happy,
All the world seems bright and gay,

And when Irish eyes are smiling,
Sure, they steal your heart away.

❀

For your smile is a part,
Of the love in your heart,
And it makes even sunshine more bright,
Like the linnet's sweet song,
Crooning all the day long,
Comes your laughter and light,
For the springtime of life,
Is the sweetest of all,
There is ne'er a real care or regret,
And while springtime is ours,
Throughout all of youth's hours,
Let us smile each chance we get.

❀

Chorus

White Wings

By Banks Winter

Sail! Home, as straight as an arrow,
My yacht shoots along on the crest of the sea,
Sail! Home, to sweet Maggie Darrow,
In her dear little home,
She is waiting for me.

High up, where cliffs they are craggy,
There's where, the girl of my heart waits for me,
Heigh, ho, I long for you, Maggie,
I'll spread out my white wings,
And sail home to thee.

Yo! Ho, how we go!
Oh! How the winds blow!
White wings they never grow weary,
They carry me cheerily over the sea,
Night comes, I long for my dearie,
I'll spread out my white wings,
And sail home to thee.

Where the River Shannon Flows

By James I. Russell

There's a pretty spot in Ireland,
I always claim for my land,
Where the fairies and the blarney,
Will never, never die,
It's the land of the shillelagh,
My heart goes back there daily,
To the girl I left behind me,
When we kissed and said goodbye.

Chorus:
Where dear old Shannon's flowing,
Where the three-leaved shamrock's grows,
Where my heart is I am going,
To my little Irish rose,
And the moment that I meet her,
With a hug and kiss I'll greet her,
For there's not a colleen sweeter,
Where the River Shannon flows.

Sure no letter I'll be mailing,
For soon will I be sailing,
And I'll bless the ship that takes me,
To my dear old Erin's shore,
There I'll settle down forever,
I'll leave the old sod never,
And I'll whisper to my sweetheart,
"Come and take my name ashore."

❀

Chorus

Believe Me,
If All Those Endearing
Young Charms

By Thomas Moore

Believe me, if all those endearing young charms,
  Which I gaze on so fondly today,
Were to change by tomorrow and fleet in my arms,
  Like fairy gifts fading way,
Thou wouldst still be adored, as this moment thou art,
  Let thy loveliness fade as it will,
And around the dear ruin, each wish of my heart,
  Would entwine itself verdantly still.

It is not while beauty and youth are thine own,
  And thy cheeks unprofaned by a tear,
That the fervor and fair of a soul can be known,
  To which time will be make thee more dear,
No, the heart that has truly loved never forgets,
  But as truly loves on to the close,
As the sunflower turns on her god when she sets,
  The same look which she turn'd when he rose.

Dear Harp of My Country

By Thomas Moore

Dear Harp of my Country! In darkness I found thee,
The cold chain of silence had hung o'er thee long,
When proudly, my own Island Harp, I unbound thee,
And gave all thy chords to light, freedom, and song,
The warm lay of love and the light note of gladness,
Have waken'd thy fondest, the liveliest thrill,
But, so oft hast thou echoed the deep sigh of sadness,
That ev'n in thy mirth it will steal from thee still.

Dear Harp of my Country! Farewell to thy numbers,
This sweet wreath of song is the last we shall twine,
Go, sleep with the sunshine of Fame on thy slumbers,
Till touch'd by some hand less unworthy than mine,
If the pulse of the patriot, solider, or lover,
Have throbb'd at our lay, 'tis thy glory alone,
I was but as the wind, passing heedlessly over,
And all the wild sweetness I wak'd was thy own.

'Tis the Last Rose of Summer

By Thomas Moore

'Tis the last rose of Summer,
Left blooming alone,
All her lovely companions,
Are faded and gone,
No flower of her kindred,
No rosebud is nigh,
To reflect back her blushes,
Or give sigh for sigh.

❀

I'll not leave thee, thou lone one,
To pine on the stem,
Since the lovely are sleeping,
Go, sleep thou with them,
Thus kindly I scatter,
Thy leaves o'er the bed,
Where thy mates of the garden,
Lie scentless and dead.

❀

So soon may I follow,
When friendships decay,

And from Love's shining circle,
The gems drop away,
When true hearts lie wither'd,
And fond ones are flown,
Oh! Who would inhabit,
This bleak world alone?

The Minstrel-Boy

By Thomas Moore

The Minstrel-Boy to the war is gone,
In the ranks of death you'll find him,
His father's sword he has girded on,
And his wild harp slung behind him,
"Land of song!" said the warrior-bard,
"Tho' all the world betrays thee,
One sword, at least, thy rights shall guard,
One faithful harp shall praise thee!"

❧

The Minstrel fell! But the foeman's chain,
Could not bring his proud soul under,
The harp he lov'd ne'er spoke again,
For he tore its chords asunder,
And said, "No chains shall sully thee,
Thou soul of love and bravery,
Thy songs were made for the pure and free,
They shall never sound in slavery."

CHAPTER

2

FAVORITE SCOTTISH SONGS

ALMOST everyone knows at least one verse of a song by Scotland's national poet Robert Burns, and it's usually the first verse of his immortal "Auld Lang Syne" (page 41). Burns (1759-1796) wrote about many themes. To this day "My Love is Like a Red, Red Rose" (page 61) is sung at weddings, and his many other songs of good cheer and conviviality are heard at gatherings in Scotland and elsewhere.

Burns also crafted the definitive versions of many Scottish legends, such as "MacPherson's Farewell" (also known as "MacPherson's Rant" and "MacPherson's Lament") (page 56) in which a rebellious man taunts the oppressors who have condemned him to die for a crime of which he is innocent, playing one last tune on the scaffold before he breaks his fiddle and prepares to meet his fate.

The poets and songsmiths who came after Burns gave us many other songs still sung today: "My Bonnie Lies Over the Ocean" (page 59) was even recorded by the Beatles in their early days, and Thomas Pattison's "The Praise of Islay" remains a lyric of surpassing beauty, a tribute to one of the most beloved of Scotland's many isles. Pattison translated the words from the ancient Scots Gaelic tongue, creating an English language masterpiece in the process. Other writers, such as Lewis Carroll and Rudyard Kipling took inspiration from "Bonnie Dundee" (page 45), and produced memorable parodies, which we've included for good measure.

AULD LANG SYNE

By Robert Burns

Should old acquaintance be forgot,
And never brought to mind,
Should old acquaintance be forgot,
And auld lang syne?

Chorus:
For auld lang syne, my dear,
For auld lang syne,
We'll take a cup o' kindness yet,
For auld lang syne.

And surely you'll be (buy) your pint stowp (cup),
And surely I'll be mine,
And we'll take a cup of kindness yet,
For auld lang syne.

Chorus

We twa hae run about the braes,
And pou'd the gowans fine,
But we've wandered monie a weary fit,
Sin' auld lang syne.

❀

Chorus

❀

We twa hae paddled in the burn,
Frae morning sun till dine (dinner time),
But seas between us braid hae roared,
Sin' auld lang syne.

❀

Chorus

❀

And there's a hand my trusty fiere (friend)!
And gie's a hand o' thine!
And we'll take a right guid-willie waught
(good-will draught),
For auld lang syne.

❀

Chorus

THE BLUEBELL OF SCOTLAND

The rose, summer's emblem,
'Tis England's chosen tree,
And France decks her shield,
With the stately Fleur-de-lis,
But brighter, fairer far than these,
There blooms a flower for me,
'Tis the Bluebell, the Bluebell,
On Scotland's grassy lea,
Where from the dark, up springs the lark,
The rising sun to see!
Where from the dark, up springs the lark,
The rising sun to see!
My land! Native land!

Where afar my steps have been,
Blue skies charm the eyes,
And the earth is ever green,
Yet dwelt my heart 'mid Scotland's glens,
Where aye in thought was seen,
The Bluebell, the Bluebell,
Amid the bracken green,
And brighter far than sun or star,
The eyes of Bonnie Jean!

And brighter far than sun or star,
    The eyes of Bonnie Jean!

❈

The Thistle, Scotland's badge,
    Up from Freedom's soil it grew,
Her foes I found it hedg'd round,
    With Rosemarie and Rue,
And, emblem that her daughters,
    Were modest, leal, and true,
From off the rocks, to deck their locks,
    They pluck'd the Bell of Blue!
The Heathbell, the Harehell,
    Old Scotland's Bell of Blue!
The Heathbell, the Harebell,
    Old Scotland's Bell of Blue!

BONNIE DUNDEE

Tae the lairds i' convention t'was Claverhouse spoke,
E'er the Kings crown go down,
There'll be crowns to be broke,
Then let each cavalier who loves honour and me,
Come follow the bonnet o' Bonnie Dundee.

Chorus:
Come fill up my cup, come fill up my can,
Saddle my horses and call out my men,
And it's Ho! For the west port and let us gae free,
And we'll follow the bonnets o' Bonnie Dundee!

Dundee he is mounted, he rides doon the street,
The bells they ring backwards, the drums they are beat,
But the Provost, douce man, says "Just e'en let him be,
For the toon is well rid of that de'il o' Dundee."

Chorus

There are hills beyond Pentland and lands beyond Forth,
Be there lairds i' the south, there are chiefs i' the north!
There are brave duniwassals, three thousand times three,
Will cry "Hoy!" for the bonnets o' Bonnie Dundee.

Then awa' to the hills, to the lea, to the rocks,
E'er I own a usurper, I'll couch wi' the fox!
Then tremble, false Whigs, in the midst o' your glee,
Ye ha' no seen the last o' my bonnets and me.

❦

Chorus

BONNIE DUNDEE (PARODY)

By Lewis Carroll (from *Through the Looking Glass*)

To the Looking-Glass world it was Alice that said,
"I've a scepter in hand, I've a crown on my head,
Let the Looking-Glass creatures, whatever they be,
Come dine with the Red Queen, the White Queen,
And Me!"

❧

Then fill up the glasses as quick as you can,
And sprinkle the table with buttons and bran,
Put cats in the coffee, and mice in the tea,
And welcome Queen Alice with thirty-times-three!

❧

"O Looking-Glass creatures," quoth Alice, "draw near!"
'Tis an honour to see me, a favor to hear,
'Tis a privilege high to have dinner and tea,
Along with the Red Queen, the White Queen,
And Me!"

❧

Then fill up the glasses with treacle and ink,
Or anything else that is pleasant to drink,
Mix sand with the cider, and wool with the wine,
And welcome Queen Alice with ninety-times-nine!

THE PARADE OF
THE PACK ANIMALS
(PARODY OF BONNIE DUNDEE)

By Rudyard Kipling (from *The Jungle Book*)

By the brand on my shoulder, the finest of tunes,
Is played by the Lancers, Hussars, and Dragoons,
And it's sweeter than "Stables" or "Water" to me,
The Cavalry Canter of "Bonnie Dundee!"

Then feed us and break us and handle and groom,
And give us good riders and plenty of room,
And launch us in column of squadron and see,
The way of the war-horse to "Bonnie Dundee!"

THE CAMPBELLS ARE COMIN'

Chorus:
The Campbells are comin', Oho! Oho!
The Campbells are comin', Oho! Oho!
The Campbells are comin', to bonnie Lochleven,
The Campbells are comin', Oho! Oho!

Upon the Lomonds I lay, I lay,
Upon the Lomonds I lay, I lay,
I looked down to bonnie Lochleven,
And saw three bonnie perches play.

Chorus

Great Argyle he goes before,
He makes his cannons and guns to roar,
Wi' sound of trumpet, pipe and drum,
The Campbells are comin', Oho, Oho!

Chorus

The Campbells they are a' in arms,
Their loyal faith and truth to show,
Wi banners rattling in the wind,
The Campbells are comin', Oho, Oho!

Chorus

COMIN' THRO' THE RYE

Gin a body meet a body,
Comin' thro' the rye,
Gin a body kiss a body,
Need a body cry?

❀

Chorus:
Ilka lassie has her laddie,
Nane, they say, hae I,
Yet a' the lads they smile at me,
When comin' through the rye.

❀

Gin a body meet a body,
Comin' from the town,
Gin a body kiss a body,
Need a body frown?

❀

Chorus

❀

'Mang the train there is a swain,
I dearly lo'e myself,
But what his name or whaur his hame,
I dinna care to tell.

❀

Chorus

HIGHLAND FAIRY LULLABY

I left my baby lying here,
Lying here, lying here,
I left my baby lying here,
To go and gather blaeberries.

❦

I found the wee brown otter's track,
Otter's track, otter's track,
I found the wee brown otter's track,
But ne'er a trace o' my baby, O!

❦

I found the track of the swan on the lake,
Swan on the lake, swan on the lake,
I found the track of the swan on the lake,
But not the track of baby, O!

❦

I found the trail of the mountain mist,
Mountain mist, mountain mist,
I found the trail of the mountain mist,
But ne'er a trace of baby, O!

❦

Hovan, Hovan Gorry og O,
Gorry og, O, Gorry og O,
Hovan, Hovan Gorry og O,
I've lost my darling baby, O!

THE LAIRD O' COCKPEN

The laird o' Cockpen, he's proud an' he's great,
His mind is ta'en up wi' things of the State,
He wanted a wife, his braw house to keep,
But favour wi' wooin' was fashious to seek.

Down by the dyke-side a lady did dwell,
At his table head he thought she'd look well,
MacLeish's ae daughter o' Claversha' Lee,
A penniless lass wi' a lang pedigree.

His wig was weel pouther'd and as gude as new,
His waistcoat was white, his coat it was blue,
He put on a ring, a sword, and cock'd hat,
And wha could refuse the laird wi' a' that?

He took the grey mare, and rode cannily,
An' rapp'd at the yett o' Claversha' Lee,
"Gae tell Mistress Jean to come speedily ben,
She's wanted to speak to the Laird o' Cockpen."

Mistress Jean was makin' the elderflower wine,
"An' what brings the laird at sic a like time?"

She put aff her apron, and on her silk gown,
Her mutch wi' red ribbons, and gaed awa' down.

🌼

An' when she cam' ben, he bowed fu' low,
An' what was his errand he soon let her know,
Amazed was the laird when the lady said "Na,"
And wi' a laigh curtsy she turned awa'.

🌼

Dumfounder'd was he, nae sigh did he gie,
He mounted his mare—he rade cannily,
An' aften he thought, as he gaed through the glen,
She's daft to refuse the Laird o' Cockpen.

🌼

And now that the laird his exit had made,
Mistress Jean she reflected on what she had said,
"Oh, for ane I'll get better, it's waur I'll get ten,
I was daft to refuse the Laird o' Cockpen."

🌼

Next time that the laird and the lady was seen,
They were gaun arm-in-arm to the kirk on the green,
Now she sits in the ha' like a weel-tappit hen,
But as yet there's nae chickens appear'd at Cockpen.

MACPHERSON'S LAMENT OR
MACPHERSON'S FAREWELL

Farewell ye dungeons dark and strong,
The wretch's destinie,
MacPherson's time will not be long,
On yonder gallows tree.

Chorus:
Sae rantonly, sae wantonly,
Sae dauntingly gaed he,
He played a tune and danc'd it round,
Below the gallows tree.

O, what is death but parting breath?
On many a bloody plain,
I've dared his face, and in this place,
I scorn him yet again!

Chorus

Untie these bands from off my hands,
An' gae to me my sword,

And there's no a man in all Scotland,
But I'll brave him at a word.

❀

Chorus

❀

I've lived a life of sturt and strife,
I die by treachery,
It burns my heart I must depart,
And not avenged be.

❀

Chorus

❀

Now farewell light, thou sunshine bright,
And all beneath the sky,
May coward shame distain his name,
The wretch that dares not die!

❀

Chorus

❀

There's some come here to see me hang,
And some to steal my fiddle,
But before that I do part with her,
I'll break her through the middle.

❀

Chorus

❀

He's ta'en his fiddle into both his hands,
And breaked her on his knee,
Said when I am gane no ither hands,
Shall every play on thee.

❧

Chorus

MY BONNIE LIES OVER THE OCEAN

My Bonnie lies over the ocean,
My Bonnie lies over the sea,
My Bonnie lies over the ocean,
Oh bring back my Bonnie to me.

Chorus:
Bring back, bring back,
Bring back my Bonnie to me, to me,
Bring back, bring back,
Bring back my Bonnie to me.

Last night as I lay on my pillow,
Last night as I lay on my bed,
Last night as I lay on my pillow,
I dreamed that my Bonnie was dead.

Chorus

Oh blow ye the winds o'er the ocean,
And blow ye the winds o'er the sea,
Oh blow ye the winds o'er the ocean,
And bring back my Bonnie to me.

❧

The winds have blown over the ocean,
The winds have blown over the sea,
The winds have blown over the ocean,
And brought back my Bonnie to me.

❧

Chorus

MY LOVE IS LIKE A RED, RED ROSE

By Robert Burns

O, my love is like a red, red rose,
That's newly sprung in June,
O, my love is like the melody,
That's sweetly play'd in tune.

❁

As fair art thou, my bonnie lass,
So deep in love am I,
And I will love thee still, my dear,
Till a' the seas gang dry.

❁

Till a' the seas gang dry, my dear,
And the rocks melt wi' the sun!
And I will love thee still, my dear,
While the sands o' life shall run.

❁

And fare thee weel, my only love,
And fare thee weel a while!
And I will come again, my love,
Tho' t'were ten thousand miles!

MY BONNIE MARY

By Robert Burns

Go fetch to me a pint o' wine,
And fill it in a silver tassie,
That I may drink, before I go,
A service to my bonnie lassie,
The boat rocks at the Pier of Leith,
Fu' loud the wind blaws frae the Ferry,
The ship rides by the Berwick-law,
And I maun leave my bonnie Mary.

The trumpets sound, the banners fly,
The glittering spears are ranked ready,
The shouts o' war are heard afar,
The battle closes deep and bloody,
It's not the roar o' sea or shore,
Wad make me langer wish to tarry,
Nor shouts o' war that's heard afar,
It's leaving thee, my bonnie Mary.

THE PRAISE OF ISLAY

By Thomas Pattison

Chorus:
Oh! My Island! Oh, my Isle!
Oh! My dear, my native soil,
Again the rising sun can smile,
With golden beams on Landy.

❀

I see afar yon hill, Ardmore,
The beating billows wash its shore,
But ah! Its beauties bloom no more,
For me no more in Islay.

❀

Chorus

❀

But birchen branches they are gay,
And hawthorns wave their silvered spraying,
And every bough the breezes sway,
Awakens joy in Islay.

❀

Chorus

❀

There eagles rise on soaring wing,
And herons watch the gushing spring,
And heath-cocks with their whirring bring,
　Their own delight to Islay.

※

Chorus

※

Its mavis sings on hazy bough,
Its linnet hunts the glen below,
And O, may long their wild notes flow,
　With melodies in Islay.

※

Chorus

※

The black-cock too, so glossy brave,
The ducks that cleave the moory wave,
The line of grey geese, long and grave,
　I've seen them all in Islay.

※

Chorus

※

I've heard the calf the dun cow greet,
The sportive lambkin loudly bleat,
The gentle doe trip fast and fleet,
　From shade to shade in Islay.

❧

Chorus

❧

Though Islay's shore is rocky, drear,
Early doth the sun appear,
On leafy brake and fallow dear,
And flocks and herds in Islay.

❧

Chorus

❧

Oh, my Island! Oh my Isle!
Oh, my dear, my native soil!
From thee no scene my heart can wile,
That's wed with love to Islay.

❧

Chorus

CHAPTER

3

Traditional English Songs

THE SONGS in this section are as much as 300 years old, and yet they are still sung on both sides of the Atlantic. "Black-Eyed Susan" (page 76) is from the pen of John Gay, the eighteenth century writer who gave us *The Beggar's Opera*, a 1728 "ballad opera." Gay (1685-1732) drew much inspiration from the story songs and ballads sung throughout England in his day, which circulated orally among the people, as well as on "broadsheets" sold by street peddlers.

Our knowledge of the ballads and broadsheets was greatly enhanced by Francis James Child (1825-1896), an American scholar who studied and traced the songs to their origins and compiled the most significant versions and variants. His collection, *The English and Scottish Popular Ballads,* remains the definitive work in the field, an invaluable resource for singers and scholars alike. Many of the ballads in this chapter are from this collection, including the most widespread and popular of the so-called "Child Ballads," "Barbara Allen" (page 73).

These ballads continue to inspire songwriters today. Bob Dylan based the structure of "A Hard Rain's Gonna

Fall" on "Lord Randall" (page 111), a finely etched tragic tale. Other songs in this chapter have a special history in America, such as "The Girl I Left Behind Me," which was sung by soldiers on both sides of the American Revolution, and continues to be sung today, in comic as well as sorrowful versions.

Admiral Benbow

O we sailed to Virginia, and thence to New York,
Where we watered our shipping and so weigh'd for Cork,
Full in view on the seas, seven sail we did spy,
O we manned our capstan and weighed speedily.

🌼

The first two we came up with were brigantine sloops,
We asked were those five others as big as they looked,
But turning to windward as near as we could lie,
We found them Frenchmen of war cruising hard by.

🌼

We took our leave of them, and made them quick dispatch,
And we steered out course to the island of Vache,
But turning to windward, as near as we could lie,
On the fourteenth of August ten sail we did spy.

🌼

They hoisted their pendants, their colors they spread,
And they hoisted their bloody flag on main-top-mast-head,
Then we hoisted the Jack flag at our mizzen peak,
And soon formed the line, tho' our squadron was weak.

🌼

The very next morning, the engagement was hot,
When brave Admiral Benbow, received a chain shot,

O when he was wounded to his men he did say,
"Take me up in your arms, boys, and bear me away."

❧

O the guns they did rattle, and the bullets did fly,
While brave Admiral Benbow for help loud did cry,
"To the cockpit convey me and soon ease my smart,
Should my brave fellows see me, it would soon,
Break their heart.

❧

And there Captain Kirby proved coward at last,
And with Wade played at bo-peep behind the main mast,
O there did they stand and quiver and shake,
Lest those French dogs should conquer and their,
Lives they should take.

❧

The very next morning, at break of the day,
We hoisted our topsails and so bore away,
We bore to Port Royal, where the people flocked much,
To see Admiral Benbow brought to Kingston Church.

❧

Come all you brave fellows wherever you've been,
Let us drink a health great George and his Queen,
And another good health to the girls that we know,
And a third in remembrance of Admiral Benbow.

Amazing Grace

By John Newton

Amazing grace, how sweet the sound,
That say'd a wretch like me!
I once was lost, but now am found,
Was blind, but now I see.

❀

'Twas grace that taught my heart to fear,
And grace my fears reliev'd,
How precious did that grace appear,
The hour I first believ'd!

❀

Thro' many dangers, toils and snares,
I have already come,
'Twas grace that brought me safe thus far,
And grace will lead me home.

❀

The Lord has promis'd good to me,
His word my hope secures,
He will my shield and portion be,
As long as life endures.

❀

Yes, when this flesh and heart shall fail,
And mortal life shall cease,

I shall possess, within the veil,
A life of joy and peace.
The earth shall soon dissolve like snow,
The sun forbear to shine,
But God, who called me here below,
Will be forever mine.

This hymn is English in origin, but sometime in the 19th century, an anonymous American added this verse, which has become standard:

When we've been there ten thousand years,
Bright shining as the sun,
We've no less days to sing God's praise,
Than when we've first begun.

Barbara Allen

Was in the merry month of May,
When flowers were a bloomin',
Sweet William on his death-bed lay,
For the love of Barbara Allen.

❀

Slowly, slowly she got up,
And slowly she went nigh him,
And all she said when she got there,
"Young man, I think you're dying."

❀

"O yes, I'm sick and very low,
And death is on me dwellin',
No better shall I ever be,
If I don't get Barbara Allen."

❀

"Don't you remember the other day,
When you were in the tavern,
I toasted all the ladies there,
And slighted Barbara Allen?"

❀

"O yes, I remember the other day,
When we were in the Tavern,

I toasted all the ladies there,
Gave my love to Barbara Allen."

※

He turned his pale face to the wall,
And death was on him dwelling,
"Adieu, Adieu, my kind friends all,
Be kind to Barbara Allen."

※

As she was walkin' through the fields,
She heard the death bells knelling,
And every toll they seemed to say,
"Hard-hearted Barbara Allen."

※

She looked east, she looked west,
She saw his corpse a-comin',
"Lay down, lay down the corpse," she said,
"And let me gaze upon him."

※

"O mother, mother make my bed,
O make it long and narrow,
Sweet William died for me today,
I'll die for him tomorrow."

※

Sweet William died on a Saturday night,
And Barbara died on Sunday,

Her mother died for the love of both,
And was buried Easter Monday.

❧

They buried Willie in the old church yard,
And Barbara there a-nigh him,
And out of his grave grew a red, red rose,
And out of hers, a briar.

❧

They grew and grew in the old churchyard,
Till they couldn't grow no higher,
They lapped and tied in a true love's knot,
The rose ran around the briar.

Black-Eyed Susan

By John Gay

All in the dawn the fleet was moor'd,
The streamers waving to the wind,
When black-eyed Susan came on board,
"Oh where shall I my true love find?
Tell me, ye jovial sailors, tell me true,
If my sweet William, if my sweet William,
Sails among your crew?"

Oh William, who high upon the yard,
Rocked with the billows to and fro,
Soon as her well-known voice he heard,
He sigh'd and cast his eyes below,
The cord slides swiftly thro' his glowing hands,
And as quick as lightning, and as quick as lightning,
On the deck he stands.

So sweet the lark, high poised in air,
Shuts close his pinions to his breast,
If, chance, his mate's shrill voice he hear,
And drops at once into her nest,
The noblest captain in the British fleet,

Might envy William, might envy William's,
Lip those kisses sweet.

❀

"Oh Susan, Susan, lovely dear!
My vows shall ever true remain,
Let me kiss off that falling tear,
We only part to meet again,
Change as ye list, ye winds, my heart shall be,
The faithful compass, the faithful compass,
That still points to thee."

❀

"Oh, believe not what the landsmen say,
Who tempt with doubts thy constant mind,
They'll tell thee sailors when away,
In every port a mistress find,
Yes, yes, believe them when they tell thee so,
For thou art present, for thou art present,
Wheresoe'er I go."

❀

"If to fair India's coast we sail,
Thy eyes are seen in diamonds bright,
Thy breath is Africa's spicy gale,
Thy skin as ivory so white,
Thus every beauteous object that I view,
Wakes in my soul, wakes in my soul,
Some charm of lovely Sue."

❀

Though battle call me from thy arms,
Let not my pretty Susan mourn,
Though cannon roar, yet safe from harm,
William shall to his dear return,
Love turns aside the balls that round me fly,
Lest precious tears, lest precious tears,
Should drop from Susan's eye.

❀

The boatswain gave the dreadful word,
Her sails their swelling bosom spread,
No longer can she stay on board,
They kissed, she sighed, he hung his head,
Her lessening boat unwilling rows to land,
"Adieu," she cries, "Adieu," she cries,
And waved her lily hand.

Blow Away the Morning Dew (The Baffled Knight)

Yonder comes a courteous knight,
Lustely raking ouer the lay,
He wel aware of a bonny lasse,
As she wand'ring over the way.

🌸

Chorus:
Then she sang "downe a downe, hey down derry,"
Then she sang "downe a downe, hey down derry."

🌸

"Jove you speed, fayre lay," he said,
"Among the leaves that be so green,
If I were a king, and wore a crown,
Full soon, fair lady, should thou be a queen."

🌸

Chorus

🌸

"Also Jove save you, faire lady,
Among the roses that be so red,
If I haue not my will of you,
Full soone, faire lady, shall I be dread."

🌸

Chorus

❀

Then he looked east, then he looked west,
He looked north, so did he south,
He could not finde a priny place,
For all lay in the dieul's mouth.

❀

Chorus

❀

"If you will carry me, gentle sir,
A mayde unto my father's hall,
Then you shall have your will of me,
Under purple and under paule."

❀

Chorus

❀

He set her up upon a steed,
And him selfe upon another,
And all the day he rode her by,
As though had beene sister and brother.

❀

Chorus

❀

When she came to her father's hall,
It was well walled round about,
She rode in at the wicket-gate,
And shut the foure-eared fool without.

"You had me," quoth she, "abroad in the field,
Among the corne, amidst the hay,
Where you might had your will of me,
For in good faither sire, I never said nay."

"Ye had me also amid the field,
Among the rushes that were so browne,
Where might had your will of me,
But you had not the face to lay me downe."

He pulled out his nut-browne sword,
And wiped the rust off with his sleeve,
And said, Jove's curse come his heart,
That any woman would believe!
When you have your own true-love,
A mile or twaine out of the town,
Spare not for her gay clothing,
But lay her body flat on the ground.

The Cruel Mother

There was a lady dwelt in York,
Fal the dal the di do,
She fell in love with her father's clerk,
Down by the green wood side.

She laid her hand against a stone,
Fal the dal the di do,
And there she made most bitter moan,
Down by the green wood side.

She took a knife both long and sharp,
Fal the dal the di do,
And stabbed her babes unto the heart,
Down by the green wood side.

As she was walking home one day,
Fal the dal the di do,
She met those babes all dress'd in white
Down by the green wood side.

She said, "Dear children, can you tell,
Fal the dal the di do,

Where shall I go? To heav'n or hell?"
Down by the green wood side.

❀

"O yes! dear mother, we can tell,
Fal the dal the di do,
For it's we to heav'n and you to hell."
Down by the green wood side.

The Cuckoo

Oh the cuckoo she's a pretty bird,
She singeth as she flies,
She bringeth good tidings,
She telleth no lies,
She sucketh white flowers,
For to keep her voice clear,
And the more she singeth cuckoo,
The summer draweth near.

As I was a-walking,
And a-talking one day,
I met my own true love,
As he came that way,
Oh to meet him was a pleasure,
Though the courting was a woe,
For I found him false hearted,
He would kiss me and go.

I wish I were a scholar,
And could handle the pen,
I would write to my lover,
And to all roving men,
I would tell them of the grief and woe,

That attend on their lies,
I would wish them have pity,
On the flower when it dies.

The Death of Queen Jane

Queen Jane was in labour full six weeks and more,
And the women were weary, and fain would give o'er,
"O women, O women, as women ye be,
Rip open my two sides, and save my baby!"

※

"O royal Queen Jane, that thing may not be,
We'll send for King Henry to come unto thee,"
King Henry came to her, and sate here bed,
"What ails my dear lady, her eyes look so red?"

※

"O royal King Henry, do one thing for me,
Rip open my two sides, and save my baby!"
"O royal Queen Jane, that thing will not do,
If I lose your fair body, I'll lose your baby too."

※

She wept and she wailed, and she wrung her hands sore,
O the flower of England must flourish no more!
She wept and she wailed till she fell in a swoon'd,
They open'd her two sides, and the baby was found.

※

The baby was christened with joy and much mirth,
While poor Queen Jane's body lay cold under earth,

There was ringing and singing and mourning all day,
The princess Elizabeth went weeping away.

❦

The trumpets in morning so sadly did sound,
And the pikes and the muskets did trail on the ground.

The Drowned Lover

As I was a walking down in Stokes Bay,
I met a drowned sailor on the beach as he lay,
And as I drew nigh him, it put me to a stand,
When I knew it was my own true Love,
By the marks on his hand.

☙

As he was a sailing from his own dear shore,
Where the waves and the billows so loudly do roar,
I said to my true Love, I shall see you no more,
So farewell, my dearest, you're the lad I adore.

☙

She put her arms around him, saying O! My dear!
She wept and she kiss'd him ten thousand times over,
O I am contented to lie by thy side,
And in a few moments, this lover she died.

☙

And all in the churchyard these two were laid,
And a stone for remembrance was laid on her grave,
My joys are all ended, my pleasures are fled,
This grave that I lie in is my new married bed.

Fanny Blair

Come all you young men and maidens,
Wherever you may be,
Beware of false swearing and sad perjury,
For it is by a false woman I am wounded so soon,
And you see how I am cut down in the height of,
My bloom.

&

It was last Monday morning I lay in my bed,
"A young friend came to me and unto me said,
Rise up Dennis Higgins and flee you elsewhere,
For they're now down against you for the young,
Fanny Blair."

&

Fanny Blair is a girl of eleven years old,
And if I was a-dying the truth I'd unfold,
It's I never had dealings with her in my time,
And it's I have to die for another man's crime.

&

On the day of the trial squire Vernon was there,
And it's on the green table he handed Fanny Blair,
And the oath that she swore I am ashamed to tell,
And the judge spoke up quickly you have told it well.

&

"Dennis Higgins of Branfield whither art thou flown,
That you are a poor prisoner condemned and alone,
If John O'Neil of Shane's Castle only was here,
In spite of Dawson ne'er known he'd soon set,
You clear."

❧

On the day that young Higgins was condemned to die,
The people rose up with a murmuring cry,
"Go catch her and crop her she's a perjuring whore,
Young Dennis is innocent we are very sure."

❧

One thing yet remaining I ask you my friends,
To wake me in Branfield amongst my dear friends,
Bring my body to lie in Merrylee mold,
And I hope that great God will pardon my soul.

The Girl I Left Behind

I'm lonesome since I crossed the hill,
And o'er the moorland sedgy,
Such heavy thoughts my heart do fill,
Since parting with my Betsey,
I seek for one as fair and gay,
But find none to remind me,
How sweet the hours I passed away,
With the girl I left behind me.

O ne'er shall I forget the night,
The stars were bright above me,
And gently lent their silv'ry light,
When first she vowed to love me,
But now I'm bound to Brighton camp,
Kind heaven then pray guide me,
And send me safely back again,
To the girl I left behind me.

Her golden hair in ringlets fair,
Her eyes like diamonds shining,
Her slender waist, her heavenly face,
That leaves my heart still pining,
Ye gods above oh hear my prayer,

To my beauteous fair to find me,
And send me safely back again,
To the girl I left behind me.

※

The bee shall honey taste no more,
The dove become a ranger,
The falling waters cease to roar,
Ere I shall seek to change her,
The vows we made to heav'n above,
Shall ever cheer and bind me,
In constancy to her I love,
The girl I left behind me.

I Once Loved a Lass
(The False Bride)

The week before Easter, the day being fair,
The sun shining brightly, cold frost in the air,
I went into the forest some flowers to find there,
And there I did pick my love a posy.

❀

O I loved a lass and I loved her so well,
I hated all others who spoke of her ill,
But now she's rewarded me well for my love,
For she's gone and she's married another.

❀

When I saw my love to the church go,
With bridesmen and bridesmaids she made a fine show,
And I followed on with my heart full of woe,
To see my love wed to another.

❀

The parson who married them aloud he did cry,
"All that forbid it I'd have you draw nigh,"
Thought I to myself I'd have a good reason why,
Though I had not the heart to forbid it.

❀

And when I saw my love sit down to meat,
I sat down beside her but nothing could eat,
I thought her sweet company better than meat,
Although she was tied to another.

❦

And when the bridesmaidens had dressed her for bed,
I stepped in amongst them and kissed the bride,
And wished that I could have been laid by her side,
And by that means I'd got me the favour.

❦

The men in yon forest they are asking me,
How many wild strawberries grow in the salt-sea,
And I answer them back with a tear in my eye,
How many ships sail in the forest.

❦

Go dig me a grave that is long, wide and deep,
And cover it over with flowers so sweet,
That I may lay down there and take a long sleep,
And that's the best way to forget her.

❦

So they've dug him a grave and they've dug it so deep,
And they've covered it over with flowers so sweet,
And he has lain down there to take a long sleep,
And maybe by now he's forgotten.

Jack Hall

Oh my name it is Jack Hall,
Chimney sweep, chimney sweep,
Oh my name it is Jack Hall, chimney sweep,
Oh my name it is Jack Hall,
And I've robb'd both great and small,
And my neck shall pay for all,
When I die, when I die,
And my neck shall pay for all when I die.

I have twenty pounds in store,
That's no joke, that's no joke,
I have twenty pounds in store, that's no joke,
I have twenty pounds in store,
And I'll rob for twenty more,
And my neck shall pay for all,
When I die, when I die,
And my neck shall pay for all when I die.

O they tell me that in jail,
I shall die, I shall die,
O they tell me that in jail, I shall die,
O they tell me that in jail,
I shall drink no more brown ale,

But be dash'd if ever I fail,
Til I die, til I die,
But be dash'd if ever I fail till I die.

❀

O I rode up Tyburn Hill,
In a cart, in a cart,
O I rode up Tyburn Hill in a cart,
O I rode up Tyburn Hill,
And 'twas there I made my will,
Saying, "The best of friends must part,
So, farewell, so, farewell."
Saying, "The best of friends must part,
So, farewell."

❀

Up the ladder I did grope,
That's no joke, that's no joke,
Up the ladder I did grope, that's no joke,
Up the ladder I did grope,
And the hangman spread the rope,
O but never a word said I,
Coming down, coming down,
O never a word said I coming down.

John Barleycorn

By Robert Burns

There was three kings into the east,
Three kings both great and high,
And they hae sworn a solemn oath,
John Barleycorn should die.

❀

They took a plough and plough'd him down,
Put clods upon his head,
And they hae sworn a solemn oath,
John Barleycorn was dead.

❀

But the cheerful Spring came kindly on,
And show'rs began to fall,
John Barleycorn got up again,
And sore surpris'd them all.

❀

The sultry suns of Summer came,
And he grew thick and strong,
His head well arm'd wi pointed spears,
That no one should him wrong.

❀

The sober Autumn enter'd mild,
When he grew wan and pale,
His bendin' joints and drooping head,
Show'd he began to fail,
His color sicken'd more and more,
He faded into age,
And then his enemies began,
To show their deadly rage.

❧

They've taen a weapon, long and sharp,
And cut him by the knee,
They ty'd him fast upon a cart,
Like a rogue for forgerie.

❧

They laid him down upon his back,
And cudgell'd him full sore,
They hung him up before the storm,
And turn'd him o'er and o'er.

❧

They filled up a darksome pit,
With water to the brim,
They heav'd in John Barleycorn,
There, let him sink or swim!

❧

They laid him upon the floor,
To work him farther woe,

And still, as signs of life appear'd,
They tossed him to and fro.

❧

They wasted o'er a scorching flame,
The marrow of his bones,
But a miller us'd him worst of all,
For he crush'd him between two stones.

❧

And they hae taen his very hero blood,
And drank it round and round,
And still the more and more they drank,
Their joy did more abound.

❧

John Barleycorn was a hero bold,
Of noble enterprise,
For if you do but taste his blood,
'Twill make your courage rise.

❧

'Twill make a man forget his woe,
'Twill heighten all his joy,
'Twill make the widow's heart to sing,
Though the tear were in her eye.

❧

Then let us toast John Barleycorn,
Each man a glass in hand,
And may his great posterity,
Ne'er fail in old Scotland!

Lord Bateman

Lord Bateman was a noble lord,
A noble lord of high degree,
He shipp'd himself all aboard a great ship,
Some foreign country to go and see.

Ⓢ

He sailed East, he sailed West,
He sailed unto proud Turkey,
Here he was taken and put in prison,
Until his life was quite weary.

Ⓢ

And in this pris'n there grew a tree,
It grew so stout, it grew so strong,
He was chained up all by the middle,
Until his life was almost gone.

Ⓢ

The Turk he had one only daughter,
The fairest creature that ever you'd see,
She stole the keys of her father's prison,
And swore Lord Bateman she would set free.

Ⓢ

"O, have you lands, O, have you livings?
And does Northumb'rland belong to thee?

What will you give a fair young lady,
If out of prison she'll set you free?"

&

"Yes, I've got lands and I've got livings,
And half Northumb'rland belongs to me,
I'll give it all to a fair young lady,
If out of prison she'll set me free."

&

She took him to her father's cellar,
And gave to him the best of wine,
And ev'ry health that she drank unto him,
"I wish, Lord Bateman, that you were mine."

&

"For seven long years we'll make a vow,
For sev'n long years we'll keep it strong,
If you will wed with no other woman,
Then I will wed no other man."

&

She took him to her father's harbour,
She gave to him a ship of fame,
"Farewell, farewell to you, Lord Bateman,
I fear I never shall see you again."

&

Now seven long years are gone and past,
And fourteen days, well known to me,

She packed up all her gay clothing,
And swore Lord Bateman she'd go and see.

❧

And when she came to Lord Bateman's castle,
How boldly she did ring the bell, "Who's there?"
"Who's there?" Cried the young proud porter,
"Who's there, who's there, come quickly tell,
O, is this called Lord Bateman's castle?
And is his lordship here within?"
"O yes! O yes!" Cried the young proud porter,
"He has just now taken his young bride in."

❧

"You tell him to send me a slice of bread,
And a bottle of the best of wine,
And not forgetting that fair young lady,
That did release him when close confined."

Away, away went the young proud porter,
Away, away, away went he,
Until he came to Lord Bateman's chamber,
Down on his bended knees fell he.

❧

"What news, what news, my young proud porter?
What news, what news hast thou brought to me?"
"There is the fairest of all young ladies,
That ever my two eyes did see.

❧

She has got rings round every finger,
Round one of them she has got three,
She has gold enough all round her middle,
To buy Northumb'rland that belongs to thee."

❧

"She tells you to send her a slice of bread,
And a bottle of the best of wine,
And not forgetting that fair young lady,
That did release you when close confined."

❧

Lord Bateman then in a passion flew,
He broke his sword in splinters three,
"Half will I give of my father's portion,
If but Sophia have a-crossed the sea."

❧

O then up spoke the young bride's mother,
Who was never heard to speak so free,
"You'll not forget my only daughter,
If but Sophia have a-crossed the sea."

❧

"I own I made a bride of your daughter,
She's neither the better nor worse for me,
She came to me on a horse and saddle,
She may go back in a coach and three."

❧

Lord Bateman prepared another marriage,
  And both their hearts were full of glee,
"I will range no more to a foreign country,
  Now since Sophia have a-crossed the sea."

My Bonny, Bonny Boy

I once loved a boy and a bonny bonny boy,
I loved him I vow and protest,
I loved him so well, there's no tongue can tell,
Till I built him a berth on my breast.

❧

'Twas up the wild forest and through the green groves,
Like one that was troubled in mind,
I hallooed, I whooped and I blew on my flute,
But no bonny boy could I find.

❧

I looked up high and I looked down low,
The weather being wonderful warm,
And who should I spy but my own bonny boy,
Locked fast in another girl's arms.

❧

He took me upon his assembled knees,
And looked me quite hard in the face,
He gave unto me one sweet smile and a kiss,
But his heart's in another girl's breast.

❧

Now my bonny, bonny boy is across the salt seas,
And I hope he will safely return,

But if he loves another girl better than me,
Let him take her, and why should I mourn?

❁

Now the girl that enjoys my own bonny boy,
She is not to be blamed, I am sure,
For many's the long night he have robbed me of my rest,
But he never shall do it no more.

Spanish Ladies

Farewell and adieu to you, fair Spanish Ladies,
Farewell and adieu to you, ladies of Spain,
For we've received orders for to sail for old England,
But we hope in a short time to see you again.

Chorus:
We will rant and we'll rave like true British sailors,
We'll rant and we'll roar all on the salt sea,
Until we strike soundings in the channel of old England,
From Ushant to Scilly is thirty four leagues.

We hove our ship to with the wind from sou'west, boys,
We hove our ship to for to strike soundings clear,
Then filled the main topsail and gore right away boys,
And straight up the Channel our course we did steer.

Chorus

The first land we sighted was called the Deadman,
Next Rams Head off Plymouth, Start,
Portland and Wight,
We sailed then by Beachy, by Fairlee and Dung'ness,
And then bore straight away for the South Foreland light.

❦

Chorus

❦

The signal was made for the grand fleet to anchor,
We clewed up our topsails, stuck out tacks and sheets,
We stood by our stoppers, we brailed in our spanker,
    And anchor'd ahead of the noblest of fleets.

❦

Chorus

❦

Then let every man here toss of a full bumper,
Then let every man here toss off his full bowl,
We'll drink and be jolly and drown melancholy,
    With a health to each jovial and drown
        true-hearted soul.

❦

Chorus

The True Lover's Farewell

O fare you well, I must be gone,
And leave you for a while,
But wherever I go, I will return,
If I go ten thousand miles, my dear,
If I go ten thousand miles.

❀

Ten thousand miles it is so far,
To leave me here alone,
While I may lie, lament and cry,
And you will not hear my moan, my dear,
And you will not hear my moan.

❀

The crow that is so black, my dear,
Shall change his colour white,
And if ever I prove false to thee,
The day shall turn to night, my dear,
The day shall turn to night.

❀

O don't you see that milk-white dove,
A-sitting on yonder tree,
Lamenting for her own true love,
As I lament for thee, my dear,
As I lament for thee.

The river never will run dry,
Nor the rocks melt with the sun,
And I'll never prove false to the girl I love,
Till all these things be done, my dear,
Till all these things be done.

Lord Randall

"O where ha you been, Lord Randall my son?
And where ha you been, my handsome young man?"
"I ha been at the greenwood, mother, make my bed soon,
For I'm wearied wi hunting, and fain wad lie down."

"An wha met ye there, Lord Randall, my son?
An wha met you there, my handsome young man?"
"O I met wi my true-love, mother, make my bed soon,
For I'm wearied wi hunting, and fain wad lie down."

"And what did she give you, Lord Randall, my son?
And what did she give you, my handsome young man?"
"Eels fried in a pan, mother, make my bed soon,
For I'm wearied wi huntin, and fain wad lie down."

"And wha gat your leavins, Lord Randall, my son?
And wha gat your leavins, my handsome young man?"
"My hawks and my hounds, mother, make my bed soon,
For I'm wearied wi huntin, and fain wad lie down."

"And what became of them, Lord Randall, my son?
And what became of them, my handsome young man?"

"They stretched their legs out an died, mother, make my
bed soon, For I'm wearied wi huntin, and fain wad lie down."

※

"O I fear you are poisoned, Lord Randall, my son!
I fear you are poisoned, my handsome young man!"
"O yes, I am poisoned, mother, make my bed soon,
For I'm sick at the heart, and fain wad lie down."

※

"What d'ye leave to your mother, Lord Randall, my son?
What d'ye leave to your mother, my handsome young man?"
"Four and twenty milk kye, mother, make my bed soon,
For I'm sick at the heart and I fain wad lied down."

※

"What d'ye leave to your sister, Lord Randall, my son?
What d'ye leave to your sister, my handsome young man?"
"My gold and my silver, mother make my bed soon,
For I'm sick at the heart, an I fain wad lie down."

※

"What d'ye leave to your brother, Lord Randall, my son?
What d'ye leave to your brother, my handsome young man?"
"My houses and my lands, mother make my bed soon,
For I'm sick at the heart, and I fain wad lie down."

※

"What d'ye leave to your true-love, Lord Randall, my son?
What d'ye leave to your true-love, my handsome young man?"
"I leave her hell and fire, mother, make my bed soon,
For I'm sick at the heart, and I fain wad lied down."

The Farmer's Curst Wife

There was an old farmer in Sussex did dwell,
There was an old farmer in Sussex did dwell,
And he had a bad wife, as many knew well.

Then Satan came to the old man at the plough,
"One of your family I must have now"

"It is not your eldest son that I crave,
But it is your old wife, and she I will have."

"O welcome, good Satan, with all of my heart!
I hope that you and she will never more part."

Now Satan has got the old wife on is back,
And he lugged her along, like a pedlar's pack.

He trudged way till they came to his hall-gate,
Says he, here, take in an old Sussex chap's mate.

O then she did kick the young imps about,
Says one to the other, Let's try turn her out.

She spied thirteen imps all dancing in chains,
She up with her pattens and beat out their brains.

✿

She knocked old Satan against the wall,
"Let's turn her out, or she'll murder us all."

✿

Now he's bundled her up on his back amain,
And to her old husband he took her again.

✿

"I have been a tormentor the whole of my life,
But I ne'er was tormented so as with your wife."

The Gypsy Laddie

The gypsies came to our good lord's gate,
And wow but they sang sweetly!
They sang sae sweet and sae very complete,
That down came the fair lady.

❀

And she came tripping down the stair,
And a' her maids before her,
As soon as they saw her well-far'd face,
They coost the glamer o'er her.

❀

"Gae take frae me this gay mantile,
And bring to me a plaidie,
For if kith and kin and a' had sworn,
I'll follow the gypsie laddie."

❀

"Yestreen I lay in a well-made bad,
And my good lord beside me,
This night I'll lay in a tenant's barn,
Whatever shall betide me."
"Come to your bed," says Johnny Faa,
"Oh come to your bed my deary,
For I vow and I swear, by the hilt o my sword,
That your lord shall nae mair come near ye."

I'll go to bed my Johnny Faa,
   I'll go to bed my deary,
For I vow and I swear by what past yestreen,
   That my lord shall nae mair come near me.

❧

   "I'll make a hap to my Johnny Faa,
   And I'll make a hap to my deary,
   And he's get a' the coat gaes round,
And my lord shall nae mair come near me."

❧

And when our lord came home at een,
   And speir'd for his fairy lady,
The tane she cry'd, and the other reply'd,
   "She's away with the gypsie laddie."

❧

"Gae saddle to me the black, black steed,
   Gae saddle and make him ready,
Before that I either eat or sleep,
   I'll gae seek my fair lady."

❧

And we were fifteen well-made men,
   Altho' we were nae bonny,
And we were a' put down for ane,
   A fair young wanton lady.

Greensleeves

Alas, my love, you do me wrong,
To cast me off discourteously,
For I have loved you well and long,
Delighting in your company.

Chorus:
Greensleeves was all my joy,
Greensleeves was my delight,
Greensleeves was my heart of gold,
And who but my lady Greensleeves.

Your vows you've broken, like my heart,
Oh, why did you so enrapture me?
Now I remain in a world apart,
But my heart remains in captivity.

Chorus

I have been ready at your hand,
To grant whatever you would crave,
I have both wagered life and land,
Your love and good-will for to have.

Chorus

If you intend thus to disdain,
It does the more enrapture me,
And even so, I still remain,
A lover in captivity.

Chorus

My men were clothed all in green,
And they did ever wait on thee,
All this was gallant to be seen,
And yet thou wouldst not love me.

Chorus

Thou couldst desire no earthly thing,
But still thou hadst it readily,
Thy music still to play and sing,
And yet thou wouldst not love me.

Chorus

Well, I will pray to God on high,
That thou my constancy mayst see,

And that yet once before I die,
Thou wilt vouchsafe to love me.

❀

Chorus

❀

Ah, Greensleeves, now farewell, adieu,
To God I pray to prosper thee,
For I am still thy lover true,
Come once again and love me.

❀

Chorus

CHAPTER

4

SHANTIES AND SAILING SONGS

THE SAILORS of England and America long ago ceased to sing these fine songs, a proud tradition of the days of sail long since swept away by the coming of steam and diesel. And yet they live on. Few singing experiences are more satisfying than raising a chorus of a classic sea shanty among good friends. This was true back in the day as well. In *Two Years Before the Mast*, Richard Dana wrote, "The sailors' songs for capstans and falls are of a peculiar kind, having a Chorus at the end of each line. The burden is usually sung by one alone, and at the Chorus all hands join in, and the louder the noise the better. A song is as necessary to sailors as the drum and fife to a soldier. They cannot pull in time, or pull with a will, without it."

Many songs were specific to certain tasks, such as heaving up the anchor or hauling rope, and they helped make the work go more quickly. Others were sung during the sailors' rare moments of leisure in their quarters in the forecastle, and earned the name "fo'c'sle" songs. Sea songs of work and pleasure have proved remarkably resilient.

The origins of many are obscure, and many like "Aweigh, Santy Ano" (page 123) are known in various versions, depending on the nationality or experience of the sailors who sang them. Though few sailors still sing today, there were few who did not in the days of sail.

AWEIGH, SANTY ANO

From Boston town we're bound away,
Heave aweigh! Heave aweigh! Santy Ano,
Around Cape Horn to Frisco Bay,
We're bound for Californi-o.

❀

Chorus:
So heave her up and away we'll go,
Heave aweigh! Heave aweigh! Santy Ano,
Heave her up and away we'll go,
We're bound for Californi-o.

❀

She's a fast clipper ship and a bully crew,
Heave aweigh! Heave aweigh! Santy Ano,
A down-east Yankee for her captain, too,
We're bound for Californi-o.

❀

Chorus

❀

Back in the days of forty-nine,
Heave aweigh! Heave aweigh! Santy Ano,
Those were the days of the good old times,
Way out in Californi-o.

Chorus

When I leave ship I'll settle down,
Heave aweigh! Heave aweigh! Santy Ano,
I'll marry a girl named Sally Brown,
Way out in Californi-o.

Chorus

There's plenty of gold, so I've been told,
Heave aweigh! Heave aweigh! Santy Ano,
Plenty of gold so I've been told,
Way out in Californi-o.

Chorus

BLOW, BOYS, BLOW

A Yankee ship came down the river,
    Blow, boys, blow,
A Yankee ship came down the river,
    Blow, my bully boys, blow.

❀

And who do you think was the skipper of her?
    Blow, boys, blow,
And who do you think was the skipper of her?
    Dandy Jim from old Carolina,
    Blow, my bully boys, blow.

❀

And who do you think was second greaser?
    Blow, boys, blow,
And who do you think was second greaser?
    Why, Pompey Squash, that fine old sailor,
    Blow, my bully boys, blow.

❀

And what do you think they had for dinner?
    Blow, boys, blow,
And what do you think they had for dinner?
    Monkey's lights and donkey's liver,
    Blow, my bully boys, blow.

❀

And what do you think they had for supper?
Blow, boys, blow,
And what do you think they had for supper?
Hard tack and Yankee leather,
Blow, my bully boys, blow.

❀

Then blow, my boys, for better weather,
Blow, boys, blow,
Then blow, my boys, for better weather,
Blow, my bully boys, blow.

❀

What do you think was the name of this clipper?
Blow, boys, blow,
What do you think was the name of this clipper?
Blow, my bully boys, blow.

❀

The Flying Cloud, with a cranky skipper,
Blow, boys, blow,
The Flying Cloud, with a cranky skipper,
Blow, my bully boys, blow.

❀

Then up aloft that yard must go,
One more pull and the belay,
I think I heard our old man say,
Blow, boys, blow.

❀

He set more sail and give her way,
We'll hoist it high before we go,
Another good pull and make it stay,
And then we've finished for to-day.
And then we've finished for to-day,
Blow, my bully boys, blow.

The Coasts of High Barbary
(The George Aloe and
the Sweepstakes)

The *George Aloe* and the *Sweepstakes* too,
 With hey, with ho, for and nony no,
 (repeat after first line of each verse)
They were two merchant-men, a sailing for Safee,
 And along the course of Barbary.
 (repeat after second line of each verse)

❀

The *George Aloe* to anchor came,
But the jolly *Sweepstakes* kept on her way.

❀

They had not sailed leagues two or three,
 Before they spied a sail upon the sea.

❀

"O hail, O hail, you lusty gallants,
From whence is your good ship, and whither is,
 She bound?"

❀

"O we are some merchant-men, sailing for Safee,"
 "And we be French rebels, a roving on the sea."

❀

"O hail, O hail, you English dogs,"
"Then come aboard, you French dogs,
And strike down your sails!"

❦

"Amain, amain, you gallant Englishmen!"
"Come, you French swades, and strike down your sails!"

❦

They laid us aboard on the starboard side,
And they overthrew us into sea so wide,
When tidings to the *George Aloe* came,
That the jolly *Sweepstakes* by Frenchmen was tane.

❦

"To top, to top, thou little ship-boy,
And see, if this French man-o-war thou canst descry."

❦

"A sail, a sail, under your lee,
Yea, and another under bough."

❦

"Weigh anchor, weigh anchor, O jolly boatswain,
We will take this French if we can."

❦

We had not sailed leagues two or three,
But we met the French man-o-war upon the sea.

❦

"All hail, all hail, you lusty gallants,
Of whence is your fair ship, and whither is she bound?"

"O we are merchant-men, and bound for Safee,"
And we are Frenchmen, roving upon the sea.

❦

"Amain, amain, you English dogs!"
"Come aboard, you French rogues, and strike your sails!"

❦

The first good shot the *George Aloe* shot,
It made the Frenchmen's heart sore afraid.

❦

The second shot the *George Aloe* did afford,
He struck the main-mast over the board.

❦

"Have mercy, have mercy, you brave Englishmen,"
"O what have you done with our brethren on shore?"

❦

"We laid them aboard on the starboard side,
And we threw them into the sea so wide."

❦

"Such mercy as you have showed unto them,
Even the like mercy shall you have again."

❦

"We laid them aboard on the larboard side,
And we threw them into the sea so wide."

❦

Lord, how it grieved our hearts full sore,
To see the drowned Frenchmen float along the shore!

Now, gallant seamen all, adieu,
This is the last news that I can write to you,
To England's coast from Barbary.

WHAT SHALL WE DO WITH THE DRUNKEN SAILOR?

What shall we do with the drunken sailor?
What shall we do with the drunken sailor?
What shall we do with the drunken sailor?
Ear-lye in the morning?

Chorus:
Way, hay, up she rises,
Way, hay, up she rises,
Way, hay, up she rises,
Ear-lye in the morning!

Throw him in a long boat 'til he's sober,
Throw him in a long boat 'til he's sober,
Throw him in a long boat 'til he's sober,
Ear-lye in the morning!

Chorus

Put him in the scuppers with the hose pipe on him,
Put him in the scuppers with the hose pipe on him,
Put him in the scuppers with the hose pipe on him,
Ear-lye in the morning!

❦

Chorus

❦

Hoist him aboard with a running bowline,
Hoist him aboard with a running bowline,
Hoist him aboard with a running bowline,
Ear-lye in the morning!

❦

Chorus

❦

Give him a taste of the bosun's rope end,
Give him a taste of the bosun's rope end,
Give him a taste of the bosun's rope end,
Ear-lye in the morning!

❦

Chorus

HOMEWARD BOUND

Our anchor we'll weigh,
And our sails we will set,
Goodbye, fare-ye-well!
Goodbye, fare-ye-well!
The friends we are leaving,
We leave with regret,
Hurrah! My boys, we're homeward bound.

We're homeward bound,
Oh joyful sound!
Goodbye, fare-ye-well!
Goodbye, fare-ye-well!
Come rally the capstan,
And run quick around,
Hurrah! My boys, we're homeward bound.

We're homeward bound,
We'd have you know,
Goodbye, fare-ye-well!
Goodbye, fare-ye-well!
And over the water,
To England must go,
Hurrah! My boys, we're homeward bound.

Heave with a will,
And heave long and strong,
Goodbye, fare-ye-well!
Goodbye, fare-ye-well!
Sing a good chorus,
For it's a good song,
Hurrah! My boys, we're homeward bound.

Hurrah! That good run,
Brought the anchor a-weigh,
Goodbye, fare-ye-well!
Goodbye, fare-ye-well!
She's up to the hawse,
Sing before we belay,
Hurrah! My boys, we're homeward bound.

"We're homeward bound,"
You've heard us say,
Goodbye, fare-ye-well!
Goodbye, fare-ye-well!
Hook on the cat fall then,
And rut her away,
Hurrah! My boys, we're homeward bound.

NEW YORK GIRLS

As I walked out on South Street,
A fair maid I did meet,
Who asked me please to see her home,
She lived on Bleecker Street.

Chorus:
And away, you Johnny,
My dear honey,
Oh you New York girls,
You love us for our money.

I said, "My dear young lady,
I'm a stranger here in town,
I left my ship just yesterday,
From Liverpool I was bound."

Chorus

I took her out to Tiffany's,
I spared her no expense,
I bought her two gold earrings,
They cost me fifteen cents.

Chorus

❀

She said, "Come with me, dearie,
    I'll stand you to a treat,
I'll buy you rum and brandy,
    Dear, and tab-nabs for to eat."

❀

Chorus

❀

And when we reached the barroom, boys,
    The drinks was handed round,
That liquor was so awful strong,
    My head went round and round.

❀

Chorus

❀

When the drinking it was over,
    We straight to bed did go,
And little did I ever think,
    She'd prove my overthrow.

❀

Chorus

❀

When I came to next morning,
    I had an aching head,

And there was I, Jack-all-alone,
　Stark naked on the bed.

❀

Chorus

❀

I looked all around the room,
　But nothing could I see,
But a lady's shift and apron,
　Which now belonged to me.

❀

Chorus

❀

Everything was silent,
　The hour was eight o'clock,
I put my shift and apron on,
　And headed for the dock.

❀

Chorus

❀

My shipmates seein' me come aboard,
　These words to me did say,
"Well well, old chap, you've lost your cap,
　Since last you went away."

❀

Chorus

❀

"Is this the new spring fashion,
The ladies wear ashore?
Where is the shop that sells it?
Have they got any more?"

❧

Chorus

❧

The Old Man cried, "why Jack, my boy,
I'm sure I could have found,
A better suit than that, by far,
To buy for eighty pounds."

❧

Chorus

❧

So come all you bully sailormen,
Take warning when ashore,
Or else you'll meet some charming girl,
Who's nothing but a whore.

❧

Chorus

❧

Your hard-earned cash will disappear,
Your rig and boots as well,
For Yankee girls are tougher than,
The other side of Hell.

❧

Chorus

THE OX-EYED MAN

The ox-eyed man is the man for me,
He came a sailing from o'er the sea,
Heigh-ho for the ox-eyed man.

Oh, May in the garden a shelling her peas,
And bird singing gaily among the trees,
Heigh-ho for the ox-eyed man.

Oh, May looked up and she saw her fate,
In the ox-eyed man passing by the gate,
Heigh-ho for the ox-eyed man.

The ox-eyed man gave a fond look of love,
And charmed May's heart which was pure as a dove,
Heigh-ho for the ox-eyed man.

Oh, May in the parlor a-sitting on his knee,
And kissing the sailor who'd come o'er the sea,
Heigh-ho for the ox-eyed man.

Oh, May in the garden a-shelling her peas,
Now weeps for the sailor who sail'd o'er the sea,
Heigh-ho for the ox-eyed man.

BLOW THE MAN DOWN

Blow the man down, bullies, blow the man down,
Blow the man down, bullies, pull him around.

Chorus:
Wae! Hae! Blow the man down,
Give me some time to blow the man down.

Blow the man down, you darlings, lie down,
Blow the man down for fair London town.

Chorus

When the *Black Baller* is ready for sea,
That is the time that you see such a spree.

Chorus

There's tinkers, and tailors, and soldiers, and all,
They ship for sailors on board the *Black Ball*.

Chorus

When the *Black Baller* hauls out of the dock,
To see these poor fellows, how on board they flock.

❀

Chorus

❀

When the *Black Baller* gets clear of the land,
'Tis then you will hear the great word of command.

❀

Chorus

❀

"Lay aft here, ye lubbers, lay aft, one and all,
I'll none of your dodges on board the *Black Ball*."

❀

Chorus

❀

To see these poor devils, how they will all 'scoat,'
Assisted along by the toe of a boot.

❀

Chorus

❀

It's now we are sailing on th' ocean so wide,
All hands are ordered to scrub the ship's side.

❀

Chorus

❀

And now, my fine boys, we are round the rock,
And soon, oh! Soon, we will be in the dock.

❀

Chorus

❀

Then all our hands will bundle ashore,
Perhaps some will never to sea go more.

❀

Chorus

RIO GRANDE

Note: the title of this song refers to the port city of Rio Grande do Sul in Brazil. Many sailors were known to pronounce "Rio" as "Rye-O."

Were you ever in Rio Grande?
Away you Rio,
(repeat after the first line of each verse)
O were you ever in Rio Grande,
I am bound to the Rio Grande,
(repeat after the second line of each verse)
Away you Rio, away you Rio,
Fare you well, my pretty young girl,
I am bound to the Rio Grande.

❧

As I was going down Broadway Street,
A pretty young girl I chanced to meet.

❧

"Oh where are you going, my pretty maid?
Oh where are you going, my pretty maid?"

❧

"I am going a milking, sir," she said,
"I am going a milking, sir," she said.

❧

"What is your fortune, my pretty maid?
What is your fortune, my pretty maid?"

❀

"My face is my fortune, sir," she said,
"My face is my fortune, sir," she said.

❀

"What is your father, my pretty maid?
What is your father, my pretty maid?"

❀

"My father's a farmer, sir," she said,
"My father's a farmer, sir," she said.

❀

"What is your mother, my pretty maid?
What is your mother, my pretty maid?"

❀

"Wife to my father, sir," she said,
"Wife to my father, sir," she said.

❀

"Then I can't marry you, my pretty maid,
Then I can't marry you, my pretty maid."

❀

"Nobody asked you, sir," she said,
"Nobody asked you, sir," she said.

THE SAUCY SAILOR BOY

He was a saucy sailor boy,
Who'd come from afar,
To ask a maid to be the bride,
Of a poor Jack tar.

The maiden, a poor fisher girl,
Stood close by his side,
With scornful look she answered thus,
"I'll not be your bride."

"You're mad to think I'd marry you,
Too ragged you are,
Be gone, you saucy sailor boy,
Be gone you Jack tar."

"I've money in my pocket, love,
And bright gold in store,
These clothes of mine are all in rags,
But coin can buy more."

"Though black my hands my gold is clean,
So I'll sail afar,

A fairer maid than you, I ween,
  Will wed this Jack tar."

❀

"Stay! Stay! You saucy sailor boy,
  Do not sail afar,
I love you and will marry you,
  You silly Jack tar."

❀

"'Twas but to tease I answered so,
  I thought you could guess,
That when a maiden answers no,
  She always means yes."

❀

"Be gone you pretty fisher girl,
  Too artful you are,"
So spake the saucy sailor boy,
  Gone was her Jack tar.

WHISKY JOHNNY

Oh whisky is the life of man,
Oh whisky! Oh, Johnny!
Oh whisky is the life of man,
Oh whisky for my Johnny!

❀

Oh whisky makes me pawn my clothes,
Oh whisky! Oh Johnny!
Oh whisky makes me pawn my clothes,
Oh whisky for my Johnny!

❀

Oh whisky gave me a broken nose,
Here's whisky for my Johnny!
Oh whisky gave me broken nose,
If I can't get whisky, I'll have rum!

❀

I thought I heard the old man say,
Whisky Johnny!
I thought I heard the old man say,
"Oh that's the stuff to make good fun!"

❀

I thought I heard the old woman say,
"Oh whisky for my Johnny!"

I thought I heard the old woman say,
"For whisky men and women will run!"

&

Oh whisky up and whisky down!
Oh whisky! Oh Johnny!
Oh whisky up and whisky down,
I'll drink whisky when I can!

&

I thought I heard the steward shout,
"Give me whisky and I'll give you tin!"
I thought I heard the steward shout,
"If you have no whisky give me gin."

&

BELAY THERE!

CHAPTER

5

Stephen Foster Songs

STEPHEN FOSTER (1826–1864) was the first great American writer of popular songs, and the greatest American songwriter of the nineteenth century. His songs continue to bring happiness to millions, but he knew much sorrow in his lifetime, and earned little from his songs in spite of their considerable sales. "Hard Times Come Again No More" (page 198) reflects some of the travails of his short life.

Though he wrote often on Southern themes, Foster went to the South only once, in 1852, when he honeymooned in New Orleans with his wife Jane Denny McDowell, for whom he wrote "Jeanie with the Light Brown Hair" (page 195).

He spent most of his life in Pittsburgh, Cincinnati and New York City, where he died. He absorbed southern music from the traveling minstrel shows of the day, and mixed it with elements of theater music and classical art songs, creating a uniquely American fusion.

Foster was prolific, and towards the end of his short life, he was cranking out songs virtually nonstop for little money and less recognition. The Civil War hurt the market for new music, and Foster himself was drinking very heavily. Yet, out of this period of despair came one of his most enduring songs, "Beautiful Dreamer" (page 247). Foster's comic songs are well known, but here we have emphasized his romantic and poetic side.

There's a Good Time Coming

Chorus:
There's a good time coming, boys,
A good time coming,
A good time coming.

❀

We may not live to see the day,
But earth shall glisten in the ray,
Of the good time coming,
Cannon balls may aid the truth,
But thought's a weapon stronger,
Well win our battle by its aid,
Wait a little longer.

❀

Chorus

❀

The pen shall supersede the sword,
And right, not might, shall be the lord,
In the good time coming,
Worth, not birth, shall rule mankind,
And be acknowledg'd stronger,
The proper impulse has been giv'n,
Wait a little longer.

❦

Chorus

❦

War in all men's eyes shall be
A monster of iniquity,
In the good time coming,
Nations shall not quarrel then,
To prove which is the stronger,
Nor slaughter men for glory's sake,
Wait a little longer.

❦

Chorus

❦

Shameful rivalries of creed,
Shall not make the martyr bleed,
In the good time coming,
Religion shall be shorn of pride,
And flourish all the stronger,
And Charity shall trim her lamp,
Wait a little longer.

❦

Chorus

❦

And a poor man's family,
Shall not be his misery,
In the good time coming,
Ev'ry child shall be a help,

To make his right arm stronger,
The happier he, the more he has,
    Wait a little longer.

❀

Chorus

❀

Little children shall not toil,
Under, or above the soil,
    In the good time coming,
But shall play in healthful fields,
Till limbs and minds grow stronger,
And ev'ry one shall read and write,
    Wait a little longer.

❀

Chorus

❀

The people shall be temperate,
And shall love instead of hate,
    In the good time coming,
They shall use, and not abuse,
And make all virtue stronger,
The reformation has begun,
    Wait a little longer.

❀

Chorus

❀

Let us aid it all we can,
Ev'ry woman, ev'ry man,
The good time coming,
Smallest helps, if rightly giv'n,
Make the impulse stronger,
'Twill be strong enough one day,
Wait a little longer.

What Must a Fairy's Dream Be?

What must a fairy's dream be,
Who drinks of the morning dew?
Would she think to fly till she reach'd the sky,
And bathe in its lakes of blue,
Or gather bright pearls from the depths of the sea,
What must the dream of a fairy be?

❀

What must a fairy's dream be,
Who sleeps when the mermaid sings?
Would she rob the night of her jewels bright,
To spangle her silv'ry wings?
Rock'd on the wind 'bove the land and the sea,
What can the dream of a fairy be?

❀

What must a fairy's dream be,
When storms in their anger cry?
Would she madly chase in the winds embrace,
The lightning gleaming by,
Or seize on its flash with a child-like glee,
What must the dream of a fairy be?

❀

What must a fairy's dream be,
When mid-summer breezes play?
Would she proudly sail on the perfum'd gale,
To welcome the dawn of day?
I know that her visions are sportive and free,
What must the dream of a fairy be?

Stay Summer Breath

Summer breath, summer breath, whisp'ring low,
Wand'ring in the darkness, where would'st thou go?
Wilt thou not linger and perfume the night,
With the Fragrance thou'st gather'd in regions of light?
Dost sigh for the rose, would'st though visit her bower,
Or sport with the mist till the coming of day,
Or art thou seeking some modest wild flower,
Whose beauty is gone with the sun's parting ray.

Summer breath, summer breath, woo not the rose,
There lies the dew drop in blissful repose,
Nestling together, they know not of death,
Would'st waft them asunder?
Stay summer breath,
Stay for the vapours above yonder fountain,
Will shun they caresses they love not the air,
And all the wild flowers that bloom on the mountain,
Will shrink from they kiss summer breath, go not there!

Summer Longings

Waiting for the May,
Waiting for the pleasant rambles,
Where the fragrant hawthorn brambles,
With the woodbine alternating,
Scent the dewy way,
Ah! My heart is weary waiting,
Waiting for the May.

Ah! My heart is sick with longing,
Longing for the May,
Longing to escape from study,
To the young face air and ruddy,
And the thousands charms belonging,
To the summer's day,
Ah! My heart is longing,
Longing for the May.

Ah! My heart is sore with sighing,
Sighing for the May,
Sighing for their sure returning,
When the summer beams are burning,
Hope and flow'rs that dead or dying,

All the winter lay,
Ah! My heart is sore with sighing,
Sighing for the May.

&

Ah! My heart is pained with throbbing,
Throbbing for the May,
Throbbing for the seaside billows,
Or the water-wooing willows,
Where in laughing and in sobbing,
Glide the streams away,
Ah! My heart, my heart is throbbing,
Throbbing for the May.

&

Waiting sad, dejected, weary,
Waiting for the May,
Spring goes by with wasted warnings,
Moonlight evenings, sunbright mornings,
Summer comes, yet dark and dreary,
Life still ebbs away,
Man is ever weary weary,
Waiting for the May.

Mary Loves the Flowers

Chorus:
Mary loves the flowers!
Ah! How happy they!
E'en their darkest hours,
To me were bright, bright summer day.

❀

Receiving all her kisses,
Inhaling ev'ry sigh,
Ever fondly bending,
Toward the radiance of her eye,
The lily and the morning glory,
Can they, can they die?

❀

Chorus

❀

Let no elfin finger,
Blur from memory's sand,
Her name ah! Let it linger,
While my air built castles stand,
To feel her soft caressing,
Her ev'ry smile to see,
To bear her ardent blessing,
Breathed in lute-toned melody,

To die beneath her tender care,
Were life, were life to me.

Chorus

Ah! May the Red Rose Live Alway

Ah! May the red rose live alway,
To smile upon earth and sky!
Why should the beautiful ever weep?
Why should the beautiful die?
Lending a charm to ev'ry ray,
That falls on her cheeks of light,
Giving the zephyr kiss for kiss,
And nursing the dew drop bright,
Ah! May the red rose live alway,
To smile upon the earth and sky!
Why should the beautiful ever weep?
Why should the beautiful die?

Long may the daisies dance the field,
Frolicking far and near!
Why should the innocent hide their heads?
Why should the innocent fear?
Spreading their petals in mute delight,
When morn in its radiance breaks,
Keeping a floral festival,
Till night loving primrose wakes,
Long may the daisies dance the field,
Frolicking far and near!

Why should the innocent hide their heads?
Why should the innocent fear?

❀

Lulled be the dirge in the cypress bough,
That tells of departed flowers!
Ah! That the butterflies gilded wing,
Fluttered in evergreen bowers!
Sad is my heart for the blighted plants,
Its pleasures are aye as brief,
They bloom at the young years joyful call,
And fade with the autumn leaf,
Ah! May the red rose live alway,
To smile upon earth and sky!
Why should the beautiful ever weep?
Why should the beautiful die?

Molly Do You Love Me?

Molly do you love me?
Can the morning beam,
Love a lowly flowret,
Living in its gleam?
Let one gentle whisper,
All my doubts destroy,
Let my dreamy rapture,
Turn to waking joy.

&

Chorus:
Molly do you love me?
Tell me, tell me true!
Molly do you love me,
Love as I love you?

&

Tell me, by those ringlets,
By those eyes of blue,
Molly! Do you love me,
Love as I love you?
Can that voice's music,
Flow from heartless glee?
Must I read no feeling, in that melody?

❦

Chorus

❦

Ah! My heart has yielded,
To those smiles that play,
With the merry dimples,
All the live-long day,
Though the tender blossoms,
Need the summer light,
Let our hearts, united,
Brave affliction's blight.

❦

Chorus

Voice of Bygone Days

Chorus:
Ah! The voice of bygone days,
Will come back again,
Whispering to the weary hearted,
Many a soothing strain.

❦

Youthful fancy then returns,
Childish hope the bosom burns,
Joy, that manhood coldly spurns,
Then flows in memory's sweet refrain.

❦

Chorus

❦

Ah! The voice of by gone days,
Murmurs to my brain,
Till the cherish'd forms departed,
See to live again,
Weeping old-time sorrows o'er,
Smiling as in days of yore,
When each heart its burden bore,
Of love and pity, bliss and pain.

Chorus

❀

Ah! The voice of bygone days,
Bids my memory rove,
To the fair and gentle being,
Of my early love,
She was radiant as the light,
She was pure as dews of night,
And beloved of angels bright,
She join'd their bless'd and happy train.

❀

Chorus

The Spirit of My Song

Chorus:
Tell me, have you ever met her,
Met the spirit of my song?
Have her wave like footsteps glided,
Through the city's worldly throng?

❖

You will know her by a wreath,
Woven all of starry light,
That is lying mid her hair,
Braided hair as dark as night.

❖

Chorus

❖

A short band of radiant summers,
Is upon her forehead laid,
Twining half in golden sunlight,
Sleeping hair in dreamy shade,
Five white fingers clasp a lyre,
Five its silv'ry strings awake,
And bewildering to the soul,
Is the music that they make.

Chorus

Though her glances sleep like shadows,
'Neath each falling, silken lash,
Yes, at aught that wakes resentment,
They magnificently flash,
Though you loved such dewy dream-light,
And such glance of sweet surprise,
You could never bear the scorn,
Of those proud and brilliant eyes.

Chorus

There's a sweet and winning cunning,
In her bright lip's crimson hue,
And a flitting tint of roses,
From her soft cheek gleaming through,
Do you think that you have met her?
She is young and pure and fair,
And she wears a wreath of starlight,
In her braided ebon hair.

Chorus

Often at her feet I'm sitting,
  With my head upon her knee,
While she tells me dreams of beauty,
  In low words of melody,
And, when my unskillful fingers,
  Strive her silvery lyre to wake,
She will smooth my tresses, smiling,
  At the discord which I make.

❦

Chorus

❦

But of late days I have missed her,
  The bright being of my love,
And perchance she's stolen pinions,
  And has floated up above.

❦

Chorus

I Would Not Die in Spring Time

I would not die in Spring time,
When all is bright around,
And fair young flowers are peeping,
From out the silent ground,
When life is on the water,
And joy upon the shore,
For winter gloomy winter,
Then reigns over us no more.

❀

I would not die in Summer,
When music's on the breeze,
And soft, delicious murmurs,
Float ever through the trees,
And fairy birds and singing,
From morn till close of day,
No, with its transient glories,
I would not pass away.

❀

When breezes leave the mountain,
Its balmy sweet all o'er,
To breath around the fountain,
And fan our bowers no more,
With Summer flowers are dying,

Within the lonely glen,
And Autumn winds are sighing,
I would not perish then.

✿

But let me die in Winter,
When night hangs dark above,
And cold the snow is lying,
On bosoms that we love,
Ah! May the wind at midnight,
That bloweth from the sea,
Chant mildly, softly, sweetly,
A requiem for me.

Turn Not Away!

Chorus:
Turn not away!
Turn not away!
From the fond heart thou hast slighted,
Scorn not my dream,
Bright as the beam,
E'er by thy cold frown benighted,
E'er by thy cold frown benighted,
E'er by thy cold frown benighted,
Bid me not now,
Spurn every vow,
Once so confidingly plighted.

Where shall I turn,
How can I learn,
Other delights to awaken?
Ne'ever can I find,
Joy for my mind,
Hope from my heart being taken,
Hope from my heart being taken,
Hope from my heart being taken,
Vainly I'll strive,

Hope to revive,
When my thee scorned and forsaken.

❀

Chorus

❀

When I would smile,
Grief to beguile,
Peace from my breast has departed,
When I would hide,
Anguish in pride,
Sorrowing teardrops have started,
Sorrowing teardrops have started,
Sorrowing teardrops have started,
Turn not away!
Turn not away!

❀

Chorus

Sweetly She Sleeps, My Alice Fair

Chorus:
Sweetly she sleeps, my Alice fair,
Her cheek on the pillow pressed,
Sweetly she sleeps, while her Saxon hair,
Like sunlight, streams o'er her breast.

Hush! Let her sleep! I pray, sweet breeze,
Breathe low on the maple bough!
Hush! bright bird, on her window trees!
For sweetly she sleeps now.

Chorus

Sweetly she sleeps, my Alice fair,
Her cheek like the first May rose,
Sweetly she sleeps, and all her care,
Is forgotten in soft repose,
Hush! Though the earliest beams of light,
Their wings in the blue sea dip,
Let her sleep, I pray, while her dreams are bright,
And a smile is about her lip.

Chorus

Farewell! Old Cottage

Chorus:
Farewell! Old cottage,
You and I must part,
I leave your faithful shelter,
With a poor breaking heart.

&

The stranger, in his might,
Hath cast our lot in twain,
The term of our delight,
Must close in parting pain.

&

Chorus

&

Farewell! Old cottage,
Memory still enthralls,
The loved ones of my childhood,
In your time beaten walls,
Here my brother played,
In pride of health and youth,
Here my sister prayed,
In purity and truth.

❧

Chorus

❧

Farewell! Old cottage,
Oft times from afar,
Yon window light hath served me,
As a loved guiding star,
And cheered a heart that longed,
To join the household mirth,
Where happy faces thronged,
A hospitable hearth.

❧

Chorus

Once I Loved Thee Mary Dear

Chorus:
Once I loved thee, Mary dear,
O how truly!

❧

As the dewdrop bright and clear,
Born but newly,
Sparkling in the solar rays,
To the rosebud's beauty, pays tribute duly,
Tribute duly.

❧

Chorus

❧

I loved thee, when in early youth,
Lovely ever,
Virtuous pride and honest truth,
Ne'er could sever,
And thy heart was pure and bright,
As the early morning's light,
Sinning never,
Sinning never.

❀

Chorus

❀

Once I loved thee, Mary dear,
Still, God bless thee!
May ever blissful prospects cheer,
And joy caress thee,
Though I drain my cups apart,
May, like mine, a saddened heart,
Ne'ever distress thee,
Ne'ever distress thee.

❀

Chorus

❀

Youth will fleet, and age will come,
Slowly, slowly,
Death will beat its muffled drum,
Lowly, lowly,
May the passing moments roll,
Bliss eternal to thy soul,
Holy, holy,
Holy, holy.

❀

Chorus

I Would Not Die in Summer Time

I would not die in Summer time,
When hearts are light and free,
And joy is borne from every clime,
Over mountain, stream and lea,
I would not leave the friends I know,
Beguiled of hope and cheer,
To lose in burning tears of woe,
The glad time of the year.

Oh! No, I would not pass away,
When from the leafy grove,
The red bird carols all the day,
Its song of joy and love,
When merry warblers trill their notes,
From every bush and tree,
And on the breeze, an anthem floats,
Of heaven-born melody.

I would not die in Summer time,
And lie within the tomb,
When blushing fruits are in their prime,
And fields are in their bloom,
For I would reap the yellow grain,

And bind it in the sheeves,
Then die when Autumn winds complain,
Among the blighted leaves.

Laura Lee

Why has thy merry face,
Gone from my side,
Leaving each cherished place,
Cheerless and void?
Why has the happy dream,
Blended with thee,
Passed like a flitting beam,
Sweet Laura Lee?
Why has the happy dream,
Blended with thee,
Passed like a flitting beam,
Sweet Laura Lee?

❀

Far from all pleasure torn,
Sad and alone,
How doth my spirit mourn,
While thou art gone!
How like a desert isle,
Earth seems to me,
Robbed of thy sunny smile,
Sweet Laura Lee!
How like a desert isle,
Earth seems to me,

Robbed of thy sunny smile,
  Sweet Laura Lee!

❀

When will thy winning voice,
  Breathe on mine ear?
When will my heart rejoice,
  Finding thee near?
When will we roam the plain,
  Joyous and free,
Never to part again,
  Sweet Laura Lee?
When will we roam the plain,
  Joyous and free,
Never to part again,
  Sweet Laura Lee?

Willie My Brave

On the lonely seabeat shore,
A maiden fair was weeping,
Calling one who far away,
Beneath the wave was sleeping,
Thus her sad unchanging strain,
Floated ever on the main.

Chorus:
Come o'er the billow,
Ride on the wave,
Come while the wind bloweth,
Willie my brave!

He said his bark would soon return,
And with a kiss they parted,
But when a year had passed away,
She then grew weary hearted,
Oh! 'Twas sad, from day to day,
To hear the maiden's plaintive lay.

Chorus

None who knew the maiden's grief,
And saw her heart's devotion,
Would tell her of the fragile bark,
That sank beneath the ocean,
But when all hope had passed away,
Her life breathed forth its parting lay.

Chorus

Maggie By My Side

The land of my home is flitting,
Flitting from my view,
A gale in the sails is sitting,
Toils the merry crew,
Here let my home be,
On the waters wide,
I roam with a proud heart,
Maggie's by my side.

❀

Chorus:
My own love, Maggie dear,
Sitting by my side,
Maggie dear, my own love,
Sitting by my side.

❀

The wind howling o'er the billow,
From the distant lea,
The storm raging around my pillow,
Brings no care to me,
Roll on ye dark waves,
O'er the troubled tide,
I heed not your anger.

❈

Chorus

❈

Storms can appall me never,
While her brow is clear,
Fair weather lingers ever,
Where her smiles appear,
When sorrow's breakers,
'Round my heart shall hide,
Still may I find her,
Sitting by my side.

❈

Chorus

Old Dog Tray

The morn of life is past,
And evening comes at last,
It brings me a dream of a once happy day,
Of merry forms I've seen,
Upon the village green,
Sporting with my old dog Tray.

❦

Chorus:
Old dog Tray's ever faithful,
Grief cannot drive him away,
He's gentle, he is kind,
I'll never, never find,
A better friend than old dog Tray.

❦

The forms I call'd my own,
Have vanished one by one,
The lov'd ones, the dear ones have all passed away,
Their happy smiles have flown,
Their gentle voices gone,
I've nothing left but old dog Tray.

Chorus

When thoughts recall the past,
His eyes are on me cast,
I know that the feels what my breaking heart would say,
Although he cannot speak, I'll vainly, vainly seek,
A better friend than old dog Tray.

Chorus

Old Memories

Fondly old memories,
Recall round my heart,
Scenes of my early joys,
That never depart,
Warmed in their sunny rays,
Hopes brightly burn.

❀

Chorus:
Say not those happy days,
Can never return!
Say not those happy days,
Can never return!
Say not those happy days,
Can never return!

❀

Voices of tenderness,
And eyes ever bright,
Warm and true hearted friends,
May lend their delight,
But still for departed smiles,
The sad heart will yearn.

❀

Chorus

Willie We Have Missed You

Oh! Willie is it you, dear,
Safe, safe at home?
They did not tell me true, dear,
They said you would not come,
I heard you at the gate,
And it made my heart rejoice,
For I knew that welcome footstep,
And that dear, familiar voice,
Making music on my ear,
In the lonely midnight gloom.

Chorus:
Oh! Willie, we have missed you,
Welcome, welcome home!

We've longed to see you nightly,
But this night of all,
The fire was blazing brightly,
And lights were in the hall,
The little ones were up,
Till 'twas ten o'clock and past,
Then their eyes began to twinkle,
And they've gone to sleep at last,

But they listened for your voice,
Till they thought you'd never come.

❧

Chorus

❧

The days were sad without you,
The nights long and drear,
My dreams have been about you,
Oh! Welcome, Willie dear!
Last night I wept and watched,
By the moonlight's cheerless ray,
Till I thought I heard your footstep,
The I wiped my tears away,
But my heart grew sad again,
When I found you had not come.

❧

Chorus

Jeanie With the Light Brown Hair

I dream of Jeanie with the light brown hair,
Borne, like a vapor, on the summer air,
I see her tripping where the bright streams play,
Happy as the daisies that dance on her way,
Many were the wild notes her merry voice would pour,
Many were the blithe birds that warbled them o'er,
Oh! I dream of Jeanie with the light brown hair,
Floating, like a vapor, on the soft summer air.

❧

I long for Jeanie with the day dawn smile,
Radiant in gladness, warm with winning guile,
I hear her melodies, like joys gone by,
Sighing round my heart o'er the fond hopes that die,
Sighing like the night wind and sobbing like the rain,
Wailing for the lost one that comes not again,
Oh! I long for Jeanie, and my heart bows low,
Never more to find her where the bright waters flow.

❧

I sigh for Jeanie, but her light form strayed,
Far from the fond hearts round her native glad,
Her smiles have vanished and her sweet songs flown,
Flitting like the dreams that have cheered us and gone,

Now the nodding wild flowers may wither on the shore,
While her gentle fingers will cull them not more,
Oh! I sigh for Jeanie with the light brown hair,
Floating like a vapor, on the soft summer air.

Come With Thy Sweet Voice Again

Come with thy sweet voice again,
To my heart still dear,
Laden with soft, soothing pain,
Like a tear, like a tear,
Bright visions, long vanished,
Round the melodies beam,
Lulled in the lap of thy sighs,
Let me dream, let me dream.

❀

Chorus
Come again! Come with thy sweet voice again!
Come oh! Come again!
Come with thy sweet voice again!

❀

Bring not a language that tells,
How the light hours roll,
Come with the music that wells,
From they soul, from thy soul,
Come not with bright off'rings,
Cold, unhallowed and new,
Bring but thine own gentle heart,
Ever true, ever true.

❀

Chorus

Hard Times Come Again No More

Let us pause in life's pleasures and count its many tears,
    While we all sup sorrow with the poor,
There's a song that will linger forever in our ears,
    Oh! Hard Times, come again no more.

Chorus:
    'Tis the song, the sigh of the weary,
Hard times, hard times, come again no more,
Many days you have lingered around my cabin door,
    Oh! Hard Times, come again no more.

While we seek mirth and beauty and music light and gay,
    There are frail forms fainting at the door,
Though their voices are silent, their pleading looking will say,
    Oh! Hard Times, come again no more.

Chorus

There's a pale drooping maiden who toils her life away,
    With a worn heart whose better days are o'er,
Though her voice would be merry, 'tis sighing all the day,
    Oh! Hard Times, come again no more.

Chorus

❀

'Tis a sign that is wafted across the troubled wave,
'Tis a wail that is heard upon the shore,
'Tis a dirge that is murmured around the lowly grave,
Oh! Hard Times, come again no more.

❀

Chorus

Come Where My Love Lies Dreaming

Come where my love lies dreaming,
Dreaming the happy hours away,
In visions bright redeeming,
The fleeting joys of day;
Dreaming the happy hours away, (Dreaming),
Come where my lies dreaming, (My own love is sweetly),
Dreaming the happy hours away.

❀

Come where my love lies dreaming, (My own love is sweetly),
Come with a lute toned lay, (Her beauty beaming),
Come where my lies dreaming, (My own love is sweetly),
Dreaming the happy hours away,
Come with a lute, come with a lay,
My own love is sweetly dreaming,
(Come, come, come, come, come, come),
Her beauty beaming; (come, come, come, come, come),

❀

Come where my love lies dreaming,
(My own love is sweetly),
Dreaming the happy hours away,
Soft in her slumber,
Thoughts bright and free,
Dance through her dreams,

Like gushing melody,
Light is her young heart,
Light may it be,
Come where my love lies dreaming,
Dreaming the happy hours,
(Come where my love lies dreaming),
Dreaming the happy hours away,
(Dreaming),
Come where my love lies dreaming,
(My own love is sweetly),
Come with a lute toned lay,
(Her beauty beaming),
Come where my love lies dreaming,
(My own love is sweetly),
Dreaming the happy hours away,
Come with a lute, come with a lay,
My own love is sweetly dreaming,
(Come, come, come, come, come, come),
Her beauty beaming,
(come, come, come, come, come),
Come where my love lies dreaming,
(My own love is sweetly),
Dreaming the happy hours away,
Dreaming the happy hours away.

Some Folks

Some folks like to sigh,
Some folks do, some folks do,
Some folks long to die,
But that's not me nor you.

Chorus:
Long live the merry merry heart,
That laughs by night and day,
Like the Queen of Mirth,
No matter what some folks say.

Some folks fear to smile,
Some folks do, some folks do,
Others laugh through guile,
But that's not me nor you.

Chorus

Some folks fret and scold,
Some folks do, some folks do,
They'll soon be dead and cold,
But that's not me nor you.

❀

Chorus

❀

Some folks get gray hairs,
Some folks do, some folks do,
Brooding o'er their cares,
But that's not me nor you.

❀

Chorus
Some folks toil and save,
Some folks do, some folks do,
To buy themselves a grave,
But that's not me nor you.

❀

Chorus

The Village Maiden

The village bells are ringing,
And merrily they chime,
The village choir is singing,
For 'tis a happy time,
The chapel walls are laden,
With garlands rich and gay,
To greet the village maiden,
Upon her wedding day.

But summer joys have faded,
And summer hopes have flown,
Her brow with grief is shaded,
Her happy smiles are gone,
Yet why her heart is laden,
Not one, alas! Can say,
Who saw the village maiden,
Upon her wedding day.

The village bells are ringing,
But hark, how sad and slow,
The village choir is singing,
A requiem soft and low,

And all with sorrow laden,
Their tearful tribute pay,
Who saw the village maiden,
Upon her wedding day.

Comrades Fill No Glass For Me

Oh! Comrades, fill no glass for me,
To drown my soul in liquid flame,
For if I drank, the toast should be,
To blighted fortune, health and fame,
Yet, though I long to quell the strife,
That passion holds against my life,
Still, boon companions may ye be,
But comrades, fill no glass for me,
Still, boon companions may ye be,
But comrades, fill no glass for me.

❀

I know a breast that once was light,
Whose patient sufferings need my care,
I know a hearth that once was bright,
But drooping hopes have nestled there,
Then while the tears drops nightly steal,
From wounded hearts that I should heal,
Though boon companions ye may be,
Oh! Comrades, fill no glass for me.

❀

When I was young I felt the tide,
Of aspiration undefiled,

But manhood's years have wronged the pride,
My parents centered in their child,
Then, by a mother's sacred tear,
By all that memory should revere,
Though boon companions ye may be,
Oh! Comrades, fill no glass for me.

Gentle Annie

Thou wilt come no more, gentle Annie,
Like a flower thy spirit did depart,
Thou are gone, alas! Like the many,
That have bloomed in the summer of my heart.

Chorus:
Shall we never more behold thee,
Never hear thy winning voice again,
When the Spring time comes, gentle Annie,
When the wild flowers are scattered over the plain?

We have roamed and loved mid the bowers,
When thy downy cheeks were in their bloom,
Now I stand alone mid the flowers,
While they mingle their perfumes over thy tomb.

Chorus

Ah! The hours grow sad while I ponder,
Near the silent spot where thou are laid,
And my heart bows down when I wander,
By the streams and the meadows were we strayed.

Chorus

The White House Chair

Come all ye men of every state,
Our creed is broad and fair,
Buchanan is our candidate,
And we'll put him in the White House Chair.

Chorus:
Then come ye men from ev'ry state,
Our creed is broad and fair,
Buchanan is our candidate,
And we'll put him in the White House Chair.

Let all our hearts for union be,
For the North and South are one,
They've worked together manfully,
And together they will still work on.

Chorus

We'll have no dark designing band,
To rule with secret sway,
We'll give to all a helping hand,
And be open as the light of day.

❀

Chorus

❀

We'll not outlaw the land that holds,
The bones of Washington,
Where Jackson fought and Marion bled,
And the battles of the brave were won.

❀

Chorus

I See Her Still In My Dreams

While the flow'rs bloom in gladness and spring birds rejoice,
There's void in our household of one gentle voice,
The form of a loved one hath passed from the light,
But the sound of her footfall returns with the night.

❀

Chorus:
For I see her still in my dreams,
I see her still in my dreams,
Though her smiles have departed from the meadows,
And streams,
I see her still in my dreams,
I see her still in my dreams,
Though her smiles have departed from the
meadows and the streams.

❀

Though her voice once familiar hath gone from the day,
And her smiles from the sunlight have faded away,
Though I wake to a scene now deserted and bleak,
In my visions I find the lost form that I seek.

❀

Chorus

Lula is Gone

With a heart forsaken I wander,
In silence, in grief and alone,
On a form departed I ponder,
For Lula, sweet Lula is gone,
Gone when the roses have faded,
Gone when the meadows are bare,
To a land by orange blossoms shaded,
Where summer ever lingers on the air.

Chorus:
Lula, Lula, Lula is gone,
With summer birds her bright smiles,
To sunny lands have flown,
When day breaketh gladly,
My heart waketh sadly,
For Lula, Lula is gone.

Not a voice awakens the mountains,
No gladness returns with the dawn,
Not a smile is mirrored in the fountains,
For Lula, sweet Lula is gone,
Day is bereft of its pleasures,
Night of its beautiful dreams,

While the dirge of well remembered measure,
Is murmured by the ripple on the streams.

✿

Chorus

✿

When I view the chill blighted bowers,
And roam over the snow covered plain,
How I long for spring's budding flowers,
To welcome her sweet smiles again,
Why does the earth seem forsaken?
Time will this sadness remove,
At her voice the meadows will awaken,
To verdure, sweet melody, and love.

✿

Chorus

My Angel Boy I Cannot See Thee Die

My Angel boy, thou'rt nearing fast,
The end of thy brief race,
Already death's dark wing hath cast,
Its shadow o'er thy face,
Must thy ethereal spirit seek,
So soon its native sky?
Still paler grows thy beauteous cheek,
I cannot see thee die,
My angel boy, my angel boy,
I cannot see thee die,
Thou, only tie that binds my soul
To earth and bids me live.

※

Thou, only thought that comfort now,
Or future hope can give,
Thou, sole pride of my widowed heart,
Thou joyous beam to mine eye,
Ah! Must thou from thy mother part?
I cannot see thee die,
My angel boy, my angel boy,
I cannot see thee die.

I meekly bow before thy throne,
Oh! God, nor dare repine,
For thou hast but recalled thine own,
He is no longer mine,
Oh! If it be thy gracious will,
We soon shall meet on high,
For me there's hope, there's comfort still,
The spirit cannot die,
My angel boy, my angel boy,
Thy spirit cannot die.

None Shall Weep a Tear For Me

My life is like the summer rose,
That opens to the morning sky,
But, e'er the shades of evening close,
Is scattered on the ground to die,
Yet on the rose's humble head,
The sweetest dews of night are shed,
As if they wept the waste to see.

❀

Chorus:
But none shall weep a tear for me,
But none shall weep a tear for me,
But none shall weep a tear for me.

❀

My life is like the autumn leaf,
That trembles in the moon's pale ray,
Its hold is frail, its date is brief,
'Tis restless soon to pass away,
Yet when that leaf shall fall and fade,
The parent tree will mourn its shade,
The winds bewail the leafless tree.

❀

Chorus

Under the Willow She's Sleeping

Under the willow she's laid with care,
(Sang a lone mother while weeping),
Under the willow, with golden hair,
My little one's quietly sleeping.

❈

Chorus:
Fair, fair, and golden hair,
(Sang a lone mother while weeping),
Fair, fair, and golden hair,
Under the willow she's sleeping.

❈

Under the willow no songs are heard,
Near where my darling lies dreaming,
Nought but the voice of some far off bird,
Where life and its pleasures are beaming.

❈

Chorus

❈

Under the willow by night and day,
Sorrowing ever I ponder,
Free from its shadowy, gloomy ray,
Ah! Never again can she wander.

❀

Chorus

❀

Under the willow I breathe a prayer,
Longing to linger forever,
Near to my angel with golden hair,
In lands where there's sorrowing never.

❀

Chorus

Jenny's Coming O'er the Green

Jenny's coming o'er the green,
Fairer form was never seen,
Winning is her gentle mien,
Why do I love her so?
We have wandered side by side,
O'er the meadows far and wide,
Little Jenny's full of pride,
Why do I love her so?

❀

Jenny's calm and liquid eyes,
Sometimes bring a sweet surprise,
Like a change in summer skies,
Why do I love her so?
Oft her voice, so full of glee,
Wakes the saddest memory,
She is younger far than me,
Why do I love her so?

❀

Little Jenny never fears,
Hoping all from coming years,
Dashing off the passing tears,
Why do I love her so? Can I not another find,
With her sweet endearing mind,

None with Jenny's charms combined?
Why do I love her so?

Old Black Joe

Gone are the days when my heart was young and gay,
Gone are my friends from the cotton fields away,
Gone from the earth to a better land I know,
I hear their gentle voices calling "Old Black Joe."

Chorus:
I'm coming, I'm coming, for my head is bending low,
I hear those gentle voices calling, "Old Black Joe."

Why do I weep when my heart should feel no pain,
Why do I sigh that my friends come not again,
Grieving for forms,
Now departed long ago?
I hear their gentle voices calling "Old Black Joe."

Chorus

Where are the hearts once so happy and so free?
The children so dear that I held upon my knee,
Gone to the shore where my soul has longed to go,
I hear the gentle voices calling "Old Black Joe."

Chorus

Down Among the Cane-Brakes

Once I could laugh and play,
When in life's early day,
Then I was far away,
Down among the cane-brakes.

Chorus:
Down among the cane-brakes on the Mississippi shore,
Oh! Those happy days, those happy days are over!
Oh! Those happy days will come back no more!

Yes I was free from care,
All was bright summer there,
Dark days to me were fair,
Down among the cane-brakes.

Chorus

There lived my mother dear,
(Gone from this world I fear),
There rang our voices clear,
Down among the cane-brakes.

Chorus

There lived a lonely one,
Who like the rest has gone,
She might have been my own,
Down among the cane-brakes.

Chorus

Long years have glided by,
Since then I breathed each sigh,
May I return to die,
Down among the cane-brakes.

Chorus

Virginia Belle

Fairer than the golden morning,
Gentle as the tongue can tell,
Was our little laughing darling,
Sweet Virginia Belle.

❧

Chorus:
Bright Virginia Belle! Our dear Virginia Belle!
She bereft us, when she left us,
Sweet Virginia Belle!

❧

How we used to roam together,
Over the mountain, through the dell,
In the smiles of springtime weather,
Sweet Virginia Belle!

❧

Chorus

❧

She was lithe as any fairy,
Winning hearts with fairy spell,
Tripping with a footstep airy,
Sweet Virginia Belle!

Chorus

❧

While her life was in its morning,
Came a sad and solemn knell,
She was taken without warning,
Sweet Virginia Belle!

❧

Chorus

Molly Dear Good Night

Molly dear, I cannot linger,
Let me soon begone,
Time now points with warning finger,
T'wards the coming dawn.

When the noisy weary day,
Shall have toiled its cares away,
To thy side again I'll stray,
Then Molly dear, good night!

Smile away the coming morrow,
Till my sure return,
Why should fond hearts part in sorrow?
Grief too soon we learn,
Hours of bliss must come and go,
Constant pleasures none can know,
Joy must have its ebb and flow,
Then Molly dear, good night!

On thy form, with beauty laden,
All my thoughts will be,
Purer love ne'er blessed a maiden,
Than I hold for thee,

While thine eyes in beauty glance,
While thy smiles my soul entrance,
Still the fleeting hours advance,
Then Molly dear, good night!

Our Willie Dear Is Dying

Our Willie, dear, is dying, love,
And thou art far away,
His little breath is sighing, love,
And cannot last till day,
Tonight while sitting by his side,
I heard him speak of thee,
My father's coming home, he said,
with presents bright for me,
My father's coming home, he said,
with presents bright for me.

❀

Chorus:
Come with an eagle's flight,
Come like a beam of light,
Come love, come home tonight,
Our Willie dear is dying.

❀

His blooming cheeks have faded, love,
The light has left his brow,
His eyes are dim'ed and shaded, love,
You would not know him now,
And when the fever rages,
With a sad and restless moan,

His feeble voice then warns us,
There is death within that tone,
His feeble voice then warns us,
There is death within that tone.

🌺

Chorus

🌺

No grief that e'er befell me, love,
Could cause this heart such pain,
Though neighbors kindly tell me, love,
He may get well again,
But a mother's heart is watchful,
All the life has left his eyes,
Oh come tonight and weep with me before our darling dies,
Oh come tonight and weep with me before our darling dies.

🌺

Chorus

I'll Be a Soldier

❦

I'll be a soldier and march to the drum,
And lie in my tent when the night shadows come,
I'll be a soldier with knapsack and gun,
And stand to my post 'till the din of battle's done.

❦

Chorus:
Farewell! My own lov'd Jenny dear,
Still will I dream of thee where ever I may stray,
Farewell! Before the coming year,
I'll be a soldier far away.

❦

I'll be a soldier and join in the fray,
With black shining belt and a jacket of grey,
I'll face up the battle as bold as a hawk,
As gay as a lark and as steady as a rock.

❦

Chorus

❦

I'll be a soldier, "my country's" the cry,
I'll fly to defend her and conquer or die,
The land of my childhood my love and my tears,
The land of my birth and my early sunny years.

I'll be a soldier, and when we have won,
I'll come back to thee with my knapsack and gun,
I'll come with a true heart and kiss off each tear,
And linger beside thee forever Jenny dear.

❦

Chorus

Oh! Tell Me of My Mother

Tell me, tell me, gentle lady,
Many things I'd love to know,
Of my dear and tender mother,
Who departed long ago,
While she moved among the living,
Were the days all bright and fair?
Did she dwell in happy sunlight,
Or in dark clouds of care?
Was she beautiful like thee,
With thy voice of melody?
Did she love and cherish me?
Oh! Tell me of my mother!
Gentle lady, let me know,
While she journeyed here below,
Was the world her friend or foe?
Oh! Tell me of my mother!

Tell me, tell me, of my mother!
Is she roaming in the skies?
I've been dreaming all about her,
And awoke with tearful eyes,
She was bending o'er my pillow,
In a deep and earnest prayer,

And her voice was like the breathing,
Of the soft summer air,
Is the world so full of pain,
That she will not come again,
Like a sunbeam on the rain?
Oh! Tell me of my mother!
Does she know I'm here alone,
While my early friends have gone,
And my dearest memories flow?
Oh! Tell me of my mother!

Farewell Mother Dear

Chorus:
Farewell! Mother dear, I go,
Where loved ones never can be parted,
We will meet again I know,
Be not weeping and downhearted.

※

Last night I dreamed of thee,
Saying pleasant things to me,
Still again those vigils keep,
While I lay me gently down to sleep.

※

Chorus

※

Weep not mother dear for me,
When I'm laid underneath the willow,
I'll keep guard upon thy soul,
Thou hast guarded over my pillow,
Far in a radiant land,
I will join a sister band,
They are singing a sweet refrain,
I am called, Farewell! We meet again.

※

Chorus

Sweet Little Maid of the Mountain

Roaming with thee I am happy and free,
Dreaming of thee fills my heart full of glee,
Longing for thee brings a sad memory,
Sweet little maid of the mountain,
Why do I grieve when I'm left alone?
Why do I sigh when thou art gone?
We will meet when the night comes on,
Sweet little maid of the mountain?

Chorus:
We'll meet when the night comes on,
Down the glade on the leafy lawn,
We'll roam till the break of dawn,
Sweet little maid of the mountain.

Over the waters we'll gracefully glide,
I've got a bark that can weather the tide,
Out on the sea I will sit by thy side,
Sweet little maid of the mountain,
Meet me at eve in the shady glen,

There I will sing a gentle strain,
You must come to that soft refrain,
Sweet little maid of the mountain?

❦

Chorus

A Penny for Your Thoughts

A penny for your thoughts!
For I know that you are dreaming,
Love's little, wicked darts are sporting with your brain,
A penny for your thoughts!
Thro' those eyes your heart is gleaming,
Longing to welcome back the starry night again,
Over the meadows thro's the dew,
You'll wander there with I know who,
Fair are her wavy locks as vapors on the hill,
A penny for your thoughts!
On thy lips a smile beaming,
You're sighing now for Jenny Dow,
That lives beyond the mill.

❀

A penny for your thoughts!
Do you think that you will love her,
When all those burning dreaming have,
Flitted from your heart?
A penny for your thoughts!
Will a halo beam above her,
When those delusive hopes and visions bright depart?
Will all blessings then as now,
Seem to linger round her brow,

Or will they vanish like the bubbles on the rill?
A penny for your thoughts!
For your heart's a cruel rover,
'Tis beating now for Jenny Dow,
That lives beyond the mill.

※

A penny for your thoughts!
They are plain beyond concealing,
Who cannot read a sighing lover through and through?
A penny for your thoughts!
I have something worth revealing,
Fair maids though full of vows, are fickle and untrue,
Now throw those flattering hopes away,
Tomorrow's Jenny's wedding day,
One with a winning voice has gained her yielding will!
A penny for your thoughts!
On your mind a change is stealing,
What think you now of Jenny Dow,
That lives beyond the mill?

The Merry Merry Month of May

We roamed the fields and riversides,
When we were young and gay,
We chased the bees and plucked the flowers,
In the merry, merry month of May.

Chorus:
Oh, yes, with ever changing sports.
We whiled away the hours away,
The skies were bright,
Our hearts were light,
In the merry, merry month of May.

Our voices echo'd through the glen,
With blithe and joyful ring,
We built our huts of mossy stones,
And we dabbled in the hillside spring.

Chorus

We joyed to meet and griev'd to part,
We sigh'd when night came on,

We went to rest with longing heart,
For the come of the bright day dawn.

❁

Chorus

Better Times are Coming

There are voices of hope that are born on the air,
And our land will be freed from its clouds of despair,
For brave and true men to battle have gone,
And good times, good times are coming on.

❀

Chorus:
Hurrah! Hurrah! Hurrah!
Sound the news from the din of the battle booming,
Tell the people far and wide that better times are coming.

❀

Abra'm Lincoln has the army and the navy in his hands,
While Seward keeps our honor bright,
Abroad in foreign lands,
And Stanton is a man, who is sturdy as a rock,
With brave men to back up and stand the battle's shock.

❀

Chorus

❀

Now McClellan is a leader and we'll let him take the sway,
For a man in his position, he should surely have his way,
Our nation's honor'd Scott, he has trusted to his might,
Your faith in McClellan put for we are sure he's right.

※

Chorus

※

Generals Lyon and Baker and Ellsworth now are gone,
But still we have some brave men to lead the soldiers on,
The noise of the battle will soon have died away,
And the darkness now upon us will be turn'd to happy day.

※

Chorus

※

Generals Sigel and Halleck they have conquered in the West,
And Burnside, victorious, he rides the ocean's breast,
The traitors and the rebels will soon meet their doom,
Then peace and prosperity will dwell in every home.

※

Chorus

※

Captain Foote is commander of the Mississippi fleet,
For his flag he strikes and makes the traitors beat,
A quick retreat,
With iron-clad gun-boats he makes the rebels run,
While Grant makes our colors wave and glitter in the sun.

General Fremont the path-finder never lags behind,
He is gone to the mountains, new pathways to find,
His voice is for freedom, and his sword is for the right,
Then hail! Noble Fremont the nation's delight.

From the land of the Shamrock there's stuff that never yields,
For we've brave Colonel Corcoran, and gallant General Shields,
From Meagher soon we'll hear, for we know that he is true,
And stands for the honor of Red, White and Blue.

Here's health to Captain Ericsson, the Monitor and crew,
Who showed the southern chivalry,
A thing they never knew,
The Merrimac has slayed as St. Patrick did the toads,
Till Worden with the Monitor came into Hampton roads.

We are Coming Father Abraham, 300,000 More

We are coming Father Abraham,
Three hundred thousand more,
From Mississippi's winding stream,
And from New England's shore,
We leave our plows and workshops,
Our wives, and children dear,
With hearts too full for utterance, with but a silent tear,
We dare not look behind us but steadfastly before,
We are coming, Father Abraham, three hundred,
Thousand more.

Chorus:
We are coming, coming our union to restore,
We are coming Father Abraham,
With three hundred thousand more.

If you look across the hilltops that meet the northern sky,
Long moving lines of rising dust your vision may descry,
And now the wind an instant, tears the cloudy veil aside,
And floats aloft our spangled flag in glory and in pride,
And bayonets in the sunlight beam,

And bands brave music pour,
We are coming, Father Abraham,
Three hundred thousand more.

❀

Chorus

❀

If you look all up our valleys,
Where the growing harvests shine,
You may see our sturdy farmer,
Boys fast forming into line,
And children from their mothers knees,
Are pulling at the weeds,
And learning how to reap and sow,
Against their country's needs,
And a farewell group stands weeping,
At every cottage door,
We are coming, Father Abraham,
Three hundred thousand more.

❀

Chorus

❀

You have called us and we're coming,
By Richmond's bloody tide,
To lay us down for freedom's sake,
Our brother's bones beside,
Or from foul treason's savage group,

To wrench the murd'rous blade,
And in the face of foreign foes its fragments to parade,
Six hundred thousand loyal men and,
True have gone before,
We are coming, Father Abraham,
Three hundred thousand more.

❖

Chorus

Beautiful Dreamer

Beautiful dreamer, wake unto me,
Starlight and dewdrops are waiting for thee,
Sounds of the rude world heard in the day,
Lull'd by the moonlight have all pass'd away!
Beautiful dreamer, queen of my song,
List while I woo thee with soft melody,
Gone are the cares of life's busy throng.

❀

Chorus:
Beautiful dreamer, awake unto me!
Beautiful dreamer, awake unto me!

❀

Beautiful dreamer, out on the sea,
Mermaids are chanting the wild lorelie,
Over the streamlet vapors are born,
Waiting to fade at the bright coming morn,
Beautiful dreamer, beam on my heart,
E'en as the morn on the streamlet and sea,
Then will all clouds of sorrow depart.

❀

Chorus

I'm Nothing But a Plain Old Soldier

I'm nothing but a plain old soldier,
An old revolutionary soldier,
But I've handled a gun,
Where noble deeds were done,
For the name of my commander
Was George Washington,
My home and my country to me were dear,
And I fought for both when the foe came near,
But now I will meet with a slight or sneer,
For I'm nothing but a plain old soldier.

Chorus:
Nothing but a plain old soldier,
An old revolutionary soldier,
But I've handled a gun,
Where noble deeds were done,
For the name of my commander,
Was General Washington.

The friends I have loved the best have departed,
The days of my early joys have gone,
And the voices once dear,
And familiar to my ear,

Have faded from the scenes of the earth one by one,
The tomb and the battle have laid them low,
And they roam no more where the bright streams flow,
I'm longing to join them and soon must go,
For I'm nothing but a plain old soldier.

❧

Chorus

❧

Again the battle song is resounding,
And who'll bring the trouble to an end?
The Union will pout, and Secession ever shout,
But none can tell us now which will yield or bend,
You've had many Generals from over the land,
You've tried one by one and you're still at a stand,
But when I took the field we had one in command,
Yet I'm nothing but a plain old soldier.

❧

Chorus

Bring My Brother Back to Me

Bring my brother back to me,
When this war is done,
Give us all the joys we shar'd,
Ere it had begun,
O bring my brother back to me,
Never more to stray,
This is all my earnest prayer,
Thro' the weary day.

❧

Chorus:
Bring him back! Bring him back!
With his smiling healthful glee,
Bring him back! Bring him back!
Bring my brother back to me.

❧

All the house is lonely now,
And my voice no more,
In the pleasant summer eves,
Greets him at the door,
Never more I hear his step,
By the garden gate,

While I sit in anxious tears,
Knowing not his fate.

✿

Chorus

✿

Bring my brother back to me,
From the battle strife,
Thou who watches o'er the good,
Shield his precious life,
When this war has passed away,
Safe from all alarms,
Bring my brother home again,
To my longing arms.

✿

Chorus

He Leadeth Me Beside Still Waters

"He leadeth me" Oh! blessed thought!
Oh! Words with heavenly comforts fraught,
Whate'er I do,
Where e'er I be,
Still 'tis God that leadeth me.

Chorus:
He leadeth me! He leadeth me!
By his own hand he leadeth me!

Sometimes, amid scenes of deepest gloom,
Sometimes, where Eden's bowers bloom,
By waters still, over troubled sea,
Still 'tis God that leadeth me!

Chorus

Lord, I would clasp thy hand in mine,
Nor ever murmur nor repine,
Content, whatever lot I see,
Since 'tis God that leadeth me.

Chorus

Chorus

And when my task on earth is done,
When by thy grace the victory's won,
E'en death's cold wave I will not flee,
Since God, through Jordan, leadeth me.

Chorus

There are Plenty of Fish in the Sea

A lady tossed her curls,
At all who came to woo,
She laughed to scorn the vows,
From hearts though false or true,
While merrily she sang,
And cared all day for naught,
There are plenty of fish in the sea,
As good as ever were caught,
There are plenty of fish in the sea,
As good as ever were caught.

❀

Upon their lightning wings,
The merry years did glide,
A careless life she led,
And was not yet a bride,
Still as of old she sang,
Though few to win her sought,
There are plenty of fish in the sea,
As good as ever were caught.

❀

At length the lady grew,
Exceedingly alarmed,

For beaux had grown quite shy,
Her face no longer charmed,
And now she sadly sings,
The lesson time has taught,
There are plenty of fish in the sea,
But, oh, they're hard to be caught.

Kissing In the Dark

Sitting in the cozy parlor,
When the nights are long,
While the cricket 'neath the window,
Sings his dainty song,
With the one we love beside us,
And no eyes to mark,
Oh how gaily glide the hours,
Kissing in the dark,
Oh how gaily glide the hours,
Kissing in the dark.

❀

Softly then the vows we murmur,
Fall upon the air,
Little hands in ours are folded,
Gently nestling there,
Not a sweeter note of music,
Sings the morning lark,
Than is heard when lips are meeting,
Kissing in the dark,
Than is heard when lips are meeting,
Kissing in the dark.

❀

Surely then we grow much bolder,
For we know this well,
That we whisper 'neath the shadows,
All love bids us tell,
Let us bless the golden hours,
With no eyes to mark,
That we pass among the maidens,
Kissing in the dark!
That we pass among the maidens,
Kissing in the dark!

Onward and Upward!

Onward and upward our watchword shall be,
While we are laboring, Jesus, for thee,
Never desponding for thou art our Guide,
Pleasantly leading us over life's tide.

Chorus:
Onward and upward! Onward and upward!
Ever our glorious watchword shall be,
Onward and upward! Onward and upward!
While we are laboring, Jesus, for thee.

Calling thy children in flocks to thy fold,
Teach them thy kindness, more precious than gold,
Saviour, O, drive from the mind and the heart,
Every dark shadow that sin can impart.

Chorus

Watchful and earnest in all that we do,
We will be faithful and we will be true,
Kindness to others we ever will show,
Loving our enemies while here below.

❀

Chorus

❀

Strengthen us, Lord, that we never grow weak,
Teach us thy heavenly pathway to seek,
Leading us on till our journey is past,
Taking us home to thy bosom at last.

❀

Chorus

She Was All The World To Me

In the sad and mournful Autumn,
With the falling of the leaf,
Death, the reaper, claimed our loved one,
As the husbandman the sheaf,
Cold and dark day we laid her,
'Neath the sighing cypress tree,
For though nothing to another,
She was all the world to me,
For tho' nothing to another,
She was all the world to me.

❀

In the month of song and blossom,
In the month when tender flowers,
Spring from earth's maternal bosom,
Waked to life by gentle shows,
As I wandered close beside her,
'Neath the spreading greenwood tree,
"Fair," I said, "and radiant maiden,
You are all the world to me."
"Fair," I said, "and radiant maiden,
You are all the world to me."

❀

Then the rare and bright-eyed maiden,
In the month of song and flowers,
Rose-lipped and beauty laden,
Curtained by the twilight hours,
Gave her hand into my keeping,
'Neath the spreading green-wood tree,
"And," she said with eyelids drooping,
"You are all the world to me."
"And," she said with eyelids drooping,
"You are all the world to me."

❦

But there hovered near a spirit,
Darker than the bird of night,
And it touched her dropping eyelids,
Covered up her eyes of light,
Then with careful hands we laid her,
'Neath the sighing cypress tree,
And my heart with her is buried,
She was all the world to me,
And my heart with her is buried,
She was all the world to me.

CHAPTER

6

Civil War Songs

IT'S SAID that Julia Ward Howe wrote "The Battle Hymn of the Republic" in response to complaints about the irreverent and vulgar songs that Union soldiers had been known to sing while out on march. Unlike some attempts to promote morality in music, hers succeeded spectacularly, and her song became a part of American history.

By this time though, American popular song had come into their own, and fine songs of every type were being written by Stephen Foster and others who helped create uniquely American song styles popular in both the North and the South. During the war, neither side had a monopoly on good songs, and we have chosen extensively from songs sung by both the Blue and the Grey. Abraham Lincoln himself is said to have been extremely fond of that quintessential Southern melody, "Dixie's Land," (page 300), written by the Ohio-born minstrel Dan Emmett. His opinion of "The Bonnie Blue Flag," the national anthem of the Confederacy, is not known.

The best songs reflected the common heritage of Americans at the time. Some, like "Pat Murphy of the Irish Brigade," also reflected the immigrant experience. Patrick

Gilmore, the greatest bandleader of the day, contributed "When Johnny Comes Marching Home" (page 328). Many commemorate the deeds of the great generals like Sherman and Jackson, while others focus on the men in the ranks.

Here you will find Abolitionist hymns, Southern anthems, battle tales, marching songs, Rebel boasts, Yankee toasts, songs for the girls that soldiers left behind and even "Aura Lea" (page 322), which got a new lease on life in the 1950s when Elvis Presley used the melody in his version of "Love Me Tender."

Abraham's Daughter

By Septimus Winner

Oh! Kind folks listen to my song,
It is no idle story,
It's all about a volunteer,
Who's goin' to fight for glory!
Now don't you think that I am right?
For I am nothing shorter,
And I belong to the Fire Zou-Zous,
And don't you think I oughter,
I'm goin' down to Washington,
To fight for Abraham's daughter.

Oh! Should you ask me who she am,
Columbia is her name, sir,
She is the child of Abraham,
Or Uncle Sam, the same, sir.
Now if I fight, why ain't I right?
And don't you think I oughter,
The volunteers are a-pouring in,
From every loyal quarter,
And I'm goin' down to Washington,
To fight for Abraham's daughter.

They say we have no officers,
But, ah! They are mistaken,
And soon you'll see the Rebels run,
With all the fuss they're makin',
For there is one who just sprung up,
He'll show the foe no quarter,
(McClellan is the man I mean),
You know he hadn't oughter,
For he's gone down to Washington,
To fight for Abraham's daughter.

We'll have a spree with Johnny Bull,
Perhaps some day or other,
And won't he have his fingers full,
If not a deal of bother,
For Yankee boys are just the lads,
Upon the land or water,
And won't we have a "bully" fight,
And don't you think we oughter,
If he is caught at any time,
Insulting Abraham's daughter.

But let us lay all jokes aside,
It is a sorry question,
The man who would these states divide,

Should hang for his suggestion,
One country and one flag, I say,
Whoe're the war may slaughter,
So I'm goin' as a Fire Zou-Zou,
And don't you think I oughter,
I'm goin' down to Washington,
To fight for Abraham's daughter.

❀

Oh! The soldiers here both far and near,
They did get quite excited,
When from their brethren of the south,
To war they were invited,
But it was to be, it is to be,
It can't be nothing shorter,
Oh! And if they call upon this child,
I'm bound to die a martyr,
For I belong to the Fire Zou-Zous,
And don't you think I oughter?
I'm goin' down to Washington,
To fight for Abraham's daughter.

❀

I am tired of a city life,
And I will join the Zou-Zous,
I'm going to try and make a hit,
Down among the Southern foo-foos,
But if perchance I should get hit,

I'll show them I'm a tartar,
We are bound to save our Union yet,
'Tis all that we are arter.

There is one thing more that I would state,
Before I close my ditty,
'Tis all about the volunteers,
That's left our good old city,
They have gone to fight for the Stars and Stripes,
Our Union, now or never!
We will give three cheers for the volunteers,
And Washington forever.

Battle Hymn of the Republic

By Julia Ward Howe

Mine eyes have seen the glory,
Of the coming of the Lord,
He is trampling out the vintage,
Where the grapes of wrath are stored,
He hath loosed the fateful lightning,
Of his terrible swift sword,
His truth is marching on.

Chorus:
Glory! Glory! Hallelujah!
Glory! Glory! Hallelujah!
Glory! Glory! Hallelujah!
His truth is marching on.

I have seen Him in the watchfires,
Of a hundred circling camps,
They have builded Him an altar,
In the evening dews and damps,
I can read His righteous sentence,
By the dim and flaring lamps,
His day is marching on.

Chorus

❦

I have read a fiery gospel writ,
In burnished rows of steel,
"As ye deal with My contemners,
So with you My grace shall deal,"
Let the Hero born of woman,
Crush the serpent with His heel,
Since God is marching on.

❦

Chorus

❦

He has sounded forth the trumpet,
That shall never call retreat,
He is sifting out the hearts of men,
Before His judgement seat,
Oh, be swift, my soul, to answer Him,
Be jubilant, my feet,
Our God is marching on.

❦

Chorus

❦

In the beauty of the lilies,
Christ was born across the sea,
With a glory in His bosom,

That transfigures you and me,
As He died to make men holy,
Let us die to make men free,
While God is marching on.

❀

Chorus

Billy Barlow

By Edward Clifford

Good evening, kind friends,
How do you all do?
'Tis a very long time,
Since I've been to see you,
I am a volunteer,
For the Union I go,
And I'm down on Secession,
Is Billy Barlow.

Oh! Yes, I'm rough, I well know,
But a bully old soldier is Billy Barlow.

Since last I saw you,
To Richmond I've been,
And during my stay,
Mrs. Davis, I've seen,
She treated me kindly,
And smiled on me so,
Old Jeff he got jealous,
Of Billy Barlow.

Oh! Yes, I'm rough, I well know,
But the ladies all like Mr. William Barlow.

❀

Now the other night,
While out for a lark,
I lost my way,
It being quite dark,
A sentinel grabbed me,
To the guardhouse I did go,
Oh! That was too rough,
On old Billy Barlow.

❀

Oh! Yes, I'm rough, I well know,
But they should not abuse old Billy Barlow.

❀

Now I see on picket,
Every time I go out,
A nice little gal,
Her name is Lize Stout,
They say she's Secesh,
But I know that's not so,
For she'll stand by the Union,
With Billy Barlow.

❀

Oh! Yes, I'm rough, I well know,
But a very good fellow is Billy Barlow.

❈

Now, theres one thing I,
Can't help but to look at,
That is what keeps our Quartermaster,
So sleek and so fat,
It may not be good living,
But there's one thing I know,
He'd get thin on the grub,
He gives Billy Barlow.

❈

Oh! Yes, I'm rough, I well know,
But I'm used to good living, is Billy Barlow.

❈

It's down in Virginia,
At a place called Bull Run,
Where first our brave soldiers,
Their fighting begun,
It's true they got routed,
But then you all know,
It was on account of the absence,
Of Billy Barlow.

❈

Oh! Yes, I'm rough, I well know,
But a bully old soldier is Billy Barlow.

❈

Just a few words more,
Then I shall have done,
And I hope what I've said,
You'll take all in fun,
If I have not done right,
Why, please tell me so,
And I'll bid you good night,
Will Billy Barlow.

❈

Oh! Yes, I'm rough, I well know,
But I hope you'll excuse poor old Billy Barlow.

For the Dear Old Flag I Die

By George Cooper

"For the dear old Flag I die,"
Said the wounded drummer boy,
"Mother, press your lips to mine,
O, they bring me peace and joy!
'Tis the last time on the earth,
I shall ever see your face,
Mother take me to your heart,
Let me die in your embrace."

Chorus:
"For the dear old Flag I die,
Mother, dry your weeping eye,
For the honor of our land,
And the dear old Flag I die."

"Do not mourn, my mother dear,
Every pang will soon be o'er,
For I hear the angel band,
Calling from their starry shore,
Now I see their banners wave,
In the light of perfect day,

Though 'tis hard to part with you,
    Yet I would not wish to stay."

❧

Chorus

❧

"Farewell mother, Death's cold hand,
    Weighs upon my spirit breath,
Fan my pallid cheek and brow,
    Closer! Closer! To your heart,
Let me feel that you are by,
    While my sight is growing dim,
For the dear old Flag I die."

❧

Chorus

Grafted into the Army

by Henry C. Work

Our Jimmy has gone for to live in a tent,
They have grafted him into the Army,
He finally puckered up courage and went,
When they grafted him into the Army,
I told them the child was too young, alas!
At the captain's forequarters, they said he would pass,
They'd train him up well in the Infantry class,
So they grafted him into the Army.

Chorus:
Oh, Jimmy, farewell!
Your brothers fell,
Way down in Alabammy,
I though they would spare,
A lone widder's heir,
But they grafted him into the Army.

Dressed up in his unicorn, dear little chap,
They have grafted him into the Army,
It seems but a day since he sat in my lap,
But they grafted him into the Army,

And these are the trousies he used to wear,
Them very same buttons, the patch and the tear,
But Uncle Sam gave him a brand new pair,
When they grafted him into the Army.

❀

Chorus

❀

Now in my provisions I see him revealed,
They have grafted him into the Army,
A picket beside the contented field,
They have grafted him into the Army.
He looks kinder sickish—begins to cry,
A big volunteer standing right in his eye!
Oh, what if the ducky should up and die,
Now they've grafted him into the Army.

❀

Chorus

John Brown's Body

John Brown's body lies a-mouldering in the grave,
John Brown's body lies a-mouldering in the grave,
John Brown's body lies a-mouldering in the grave,
But his soul goes marching on.

Chorus:
Glory, glory, hallelujah,
Glory, glory, hallelujah,
Glory, glory, hallelujah,
His soul goes marching on.

He's gone to be a soldier in the Army of the Lord,
He's gone to be a soldier in the Army of the Lord,
He's gone to be a soldier in the Army of the Lord,
His soul goes marching on.

Chorus

John Brown's knapsack is strapped upon his back,
John Brown's knapsack is strapped upon his back,
John Brown's knapsack is strapped upon his back,
His soul goes marching on.

❀

Chorus

❀

John Brown died that the slaves might be free,
John Brown died that the slaves might be free,
John Brown died that the slaves might be free,
But his soul goes marching on.

❀

Chorus

❀

The stars above in Heaven now are looking kindly down,
The stars above in Heaven now are looking kindly down,
The stars above in Heaven now are looking kindly down,
On the grave of old John Brown.

❀

Chorus

Lincoln and Liberty

By Jesse Hutchinson

❧❧

Hurrah for the choice of the nation,
　Our chieftain so brave and so true,
We'll go for the great reformation,
　For Lincoln and Liberty, too!
We'll go for the son of Kentucky,
　The hero of Hoosierdom through,
The pride of the "Suckers" so lucky,
　For Lincoln and Liberty, too!

❧

They'll find what by felling and mauling,
　Our railmaker statesman can do,
For the people are everywhere calling,
　For Lincoln and Liberty, too,
Then up with the banner so glorious,
　The star-spangled red, white, and blue,
We'll fight till our banner's victorious,
　For Lincoln and Liberty, too.

❧

Our David's good sling is unerring,
　The Slavocrat's giant he slew,
The shout for the freedom preferring,

For Lincoln and Liberty, too,
We'll go for the son of Kentucky,
The hero of Hoosierdom through,
The pride of the "Suckers" so lucky,
For Lincoln and Liberty, too.

Marching Along

By William B. Bradbury

The army is gath'ring from near and from far,
The trumpet is sounding the call for the war,
McClellan's our leader, he's gallant and strong,
We'll gird on our armor and be marching along.

Chorus:
Marching along, we are marching along,
Gird on the armor and be marching along,
McClellan's our leader, he's gallant and strong,
For God and for country we are marching along.

The foe is before us in battle array,
But let us not waver or turn from the way,
The Lord is our strength and the Union's our song,
With courage and faith we are marching along.

Chorus

Our wives and our children we leave in your care,
We feel you will help them with sorrow to bear,

'Tis hard thus to part, but we hope it 'twon't be long,
We'll keep up our heart as we're marching along.

☙

Chorus

☙

We sigh for our country, we mourn for our dead,
For them now our last drop of blood we will shed,
Our cause is the right one—our foe's in the wrong,
Then gladly we'll sing as we're marching along.

☙

Chorus

☙

The flag of our country is floating on high,
We'll stand by that flag till we conquer or die,
McClellan's our leader, he's gallant and strong,
We'll gird our armor and be marching along.

☙

Chorus

My Maryland (Union Version)

Sung to the tune of "O Tannenbaum" or "O Christmas Tree."

The Rebel feet are on our shore,
    Maryland, my Maryland!
I smell them half a mile or more,
    Maryland, my Maryland!
Their shockless hordes are at my door,
Their drunken generals on my floor,
What now can sweeten Baltimore?
    Maryland, my Maryland!

    ❀

Hark to our noses' dire appeal,
    Maryland, my Maryland!
Oh unwashed Rebs to you we kneel!
    Maryland, my Maryland!
If you can't purchase soap, oh steal,
    That precious article–I feel,
Like scratching from the head to heel,
    Maryland, my Maryland!

    ❀

You're covered thick with mud and dust,
    Maryland, my Maryland!

As though you'd been upon a bust,
Maryland, my Maryland!
Remember, it is scarcely just,
To have a filthy fellow thrust,
Before us, till he's been scrubbed fust,
Maryland, my Maryland!

❧

I see no blush upon thy cheek,
Maryland, my Maryland!
It's not been washed for many a week,
Maryland, my Maryland!
To get thee clean—'tis truth I speak,
Would dirty every stream and creek,
From Potomac to Chesapeake,
Maryland, my Maryland!

The Army of the Free

By Frank H. Norton
Sung to the tune of "The Wearing of the Green."

In the army of the Union we are marching in the van,
And will do the work before us, if the bravest soldiers can,
We will drive the Rebel forces from their
strongholds to the sea,
And will live and die together in the Army of the Free.

❀

Chorus:
The Army of the Free, the Army of the Free,
We will live and die together in the Army of the Free.

❀

We may rust beneath inaction, we may sink beneath disease,
The summer sun may scorch us or the winter's blasts
may freeze,
But whatever may befall us, we will let the Rebels see,
That unconquered we shall still remain the Army of the Free.

❀

Chorus

❀

We are the best division of a half a million souls,
And only resting on our arms till the war cry onward rolls,

When our gallant General Porter calls,
Why ready we shall be,
To follow him forever with the Army of the Free.

❦

Chorus

❦

We have Butterfield the daring and
we've Martindale the cool,
Where could we learn the art of war
within a better school,
Add Morell to the list of names and we must all agree,
We have the finest Generals in the Army of the Free.

❦

Chorus

❦

Though we live in winter quarters now, we're waiting
but the hour,
When Porter's brave division shall go forth in all its power,
And when on the field of battle, fighting we shall be,
We'll show that we cannot disgrace the Army of the Free.

❦

Chorus

❦

Then hurrah for our Division, may it soon be called to go,
To add its strength to those who have advanced to meet
the foe,

God bless it, for we know right well, wherever it may be,
'Twill never fail to honor our great Army of the Free.

❧

Chorus

The Battle Cry of Freedom

By George F. Root

Yes, we'll rally round the flag, boys, we'll rally once again,
Shouting the battle cry of Freedom,
We will rally from the hillside, we'll gather from the plain,
Shouting the battle cry of Freedom.

Chorus:
The Union forever,
Hurrah! Boys, hurrah!
Down with the traitors,
Up with the stars,
While we rally round the flag, boys,
Rally once again,
Shouting the battle cry of Freedom.

We are springing to the call of our brothers gone before,
Shouting the battle cry of Freedom,
And we'll fill our vacant ranks with a million freemen more,
Shouting the battle cry of Freedom.

Chorus

We will welcome to our numbers the loyal, true and brave,
        Shouting the battle cry of Freedom,
And although they may be poor, not a man shall be a slave,
        Shouting the battle cry of Freedom.

Chorus

So we're springing to the call from the East and from the West,
        Shouting the battle cry of Freedom,
And we'll hurl the Rebel crew from the land that we love best,
        Shouting the battle cry of Freedom.

Chorus

The New York Volunteer

'Twas in the days of seventy-six,
When freemen young and old,
All fought for Independence then,
Each hero brave and bold!
'Twas then the noble Stars and Stripes,
In triumph did appear,
And defended by brave patriots,
The Yankee Volunteers,
'Tis my delight to march and fight,
Like a New York Volunteer!

Now, there's our City Regiments,
Just see what they have done,
The first to offer to the State,
To go to Washington,
To protect the Federal Capital,
And the flag they love so dear!
And they've done their duty nobly,
Like New York Volunteers!
'Tis my delight to march and fight,
Like a New York Volunteer!

The Rebels out in Maryland,
They madly raved and swore,
They'd let none of our Union troops,
Pass through Baltimore,
But the Massachusetts Regiment,
No traitors did they fear,
But fought their way to Washington,
Like Yankee Volunteers!
'Tis my delight to march and fight,
Like a New York Volunteer!

Tramp! Tramp! Tramp!
(The Prisoner's Hope)

By George F. Root

In the prison cell I sit,
Thinking mother, dear, of you,
And our bright and happy home so far away,
And the tears, they fill my eyes,
'Spite of all that I can do,
Tho' I try to cheer my comrades and be gay.

Chorus:
Tramp, tramp, tramp, the boys are marching,
Cheer up comrades they will come,
And beneath the starry flag,
We shall breathe the air again,
Of the free land in our own beloved home.

In the battle front we stood,
When their fiercest charge they made,
And they swept us off a hundred men or more,
But before we reached their lines,

They were beaten back dismayed,
And we heard the cry of vict'ry o'er and o'er.

❧

Chorus

❧

So within the prison cell,
We are waiting for the day,
That shall come to open wide the iron door,
And the hollow eye grows bright,
And the poor heart almost gay,
As we think of seeing home and friends once more.

❧

Chorus

When Sherman Marched Down to the Sea

By S.B.M. Meyers

Our campfires shone bright on the mountains,
That frowned on the river below,
While we stood by our guns in the morning,
And eagerly watched for the foe,
When a rider came out of the darkness,
That hung over mountain and tree,
And shouted "Boys! Up and be ready!
For Sherman will march to the sea,"
And shouted "Boys, up and be ready,
For Sherman will march to the sea."

Then shout upon shout for bold Sherman,
Went up from each valley and glen,
And the bugles re-echoed the music,
That rose from the lips of the men,
For we know that the stars in our banners,
More bright in their splendor would be,
And that blessings from North land would greet us,
When Sherman marched down to the sea,

And that blessings from North land would greet us,
When Sherman marched down to the sea.

✿

Then forward, boys, forward to battle,
We marched on our wearisome way,
And we stormed the wild hills of Resacca,
God bless those who fell on that day!
Then Kennesaw, dark in its glory,
Frowned down on the flag of the free,
But the East and the West bore our standards,
When Sherman marched down to the sea,
But the East and the West bore our standards,
When Sherman marched down to the sea.

✿

Still onward we pressed till our banners,
Swept out from Atlanta's grim walls,
And the blood of the patriot dampened,
The soil where the Traitor flag falls,
We paused not to weep for the fallen,
That slept by each river and tree,
But we twined them a wreath of the laurel,
When Sherman marched down to the sea,
But we twined them a wreath of the laurel,
When Sherman marched down to the sea.

✿

Proud, proud was our army that morning,
That stood where the pine darkly towers,
When Sherman said, "Boys, you are weary,
But today, fair Savannah is ours."
Then we all sand a song for our Chieftain,
That echoed over river and lea,
And the stars on our banners shone brighter,
When Sherman marched down to the sea,
And the stars on our banners shone brighter,
When Sherman marched down to the sea.

Dixie's Land

By Daniel Emmett

I wish I was in the land of cotton,
Old times there are not forgotten,
Look away! Look away! Look away, Dixie's Land!
In Dixie's Land where I was born in,
Early on one frosty morning,
Look away! Look away! Look away, Dixie's Land!

Chorus:
Then I wish I was in Dixie! Hooray! Hooray!
In Dixie's Land I'll take my stand, to live and die in Dixie!
Away! Away! Away down South in Dixie!
Away! Away! Away down South in Dixie!

Old Missus married "Will the Weaver,"
William was a gay deceiver!
Look away! Look away! Look away, Dixie's Land!
But when he put his arm around her,
Smiled as fierce as a forty-pounder!
Look away! Look away! Look away, Dixie's Land!

Chorus

His face was sharp as a butcher's cleaver,
But that did not seem to grieve her!
Look away! Look away! Look away, Dixie's Land!
Old Missus acted the foolish part,
And died for a man that broke her heart!
Look away! Look away! Look away, Dixie's Land!

❀

Chorus

❀

Now here's a health to the next old missus,
And all the gals that want to kiss us!
Look away! Look away! Look away, Dixie's Land!
But if you want to drive away sorrow,
Come and hear this song tomorrow!
Look away! Look away! Look away, Dixie's Land!

❀

Chorus

❀

There's buckwheat cakes and Indian batter,
Makes you fat or a little fatter!
Look away! Look away! Look away, Dixie's Land!
Then hoe it down and scratch your gravel,
To Dixie's Land I'm bound to travel!
Look away! Look away! Look away, Dixie's Land!

❀

Chorus

God Save the South

By Earnest Halpin

God save the South, God save the South,
Her altars and firesides, God save the South!
Now that the war is nigh, now that we arm to die,
Chanting our battle cry, "Freedom or death!"
Chanting our battle cry, "Freedom or death!"

God be our shield, at home or afield,
Stretch Thine arm over us, strengthen and save,
What tho' they're three to one, forward each sire and son,
Strike till the war is won, strike to the grave!
Strike till the war is won, strike to the grave!

God made the right stronger than might,
Millions would trample us down in their pride,
Lay Thou their legions low, roll back the ruthless foe,
Let the proud spoiler know God's on our side,
Let the proud spoiler know God's on our side.

Hark honor's call, summoning all,
Summoning all of us unto the strife,
Sons of the South, awake! Strike till the brand shall break,

Strike for dear Honor's sake, Freedom and Life!
Strike for dear Honor's sake, Freedom and Life!

❧

Rebels before, our fathers of yore,
Rebel's the righteous name Washington bore,
Why, then, be ours the same, the name that he
snatched from shame,
Making it first in fame, foremost in war,
Making it first in fame, foremost in war.

❧

War to the hilt, theirs be the guilt,
Who fetter the free man to ransom the slave,
Up then, and undismay'd, sheathe not the battle blade,
Till the last foe is laid low in the grave!
Till the last foe is laid low in the grave!

❧

God save the South, God save the South,
Dry the dim eyes that now follow our path,
Still let the light feet rove safe through the orange grove,
Still keep the land we love safe from Thy wrath,
Still keep the land we love safe from Thy wrath.

❧

God save the South, God save the South,
Her altars and firesides, God save the South!
For the great war is nigh, and we will win or die,
Chanting our battle cry, "Freedom or death!"
Chanting our battle cry, "Freedom or death!"

Goober Peas

By A. Pindar

Sittin' by the roadside on a summer's day,
Chattin' with my messmates, passing time away,
Lying in the shadow, underneath the trees,
Goodness, how delicious, eating goober peas!

Chorus:
Peas! Peas! Peas! Peas!
Eating goober peas!
Goodness, how delicious,
Eating goober peas!

When a horseman passes, the soldiers have a rule,
To cry out at their loudest "Mister, here's your mule!"
But still another pleasure enchantinger than these,
Is wearing out your grinders, eating goober peas!

Chorus

Just before the battle, the Gen'ral hears a row,
He says "The Yanks are coming, I hear their rifles now!"
He turns around in wonder, and what do you think he sees?
The Georgia Militia—eating goober peas!

Chorus

I think my song had lasted almost long enough,
The subject's interesting, but rhymes are mighty rough!
I wish this war was over, when free from rags and fleas,
We'd kiss our wives and sweethearts and gobble goober peas!

Chorus

Lorena

By Rev. H.D.L. Webster

The years creep slowly by, Lorena,
The snow is on the grass again,
The sun's low down the sky, Lorena,
The frost gleams where the flowers have been,
But the heart throbs on as lovely now,
As when the summer days were nigh,
Oh, the sun can never dip so low,
Adown affection's cloudless sky.

❀

A hundred months have passed, Lorena,
Since last I held your hand in mine,
And felt that pulse beat fast, Lorena,
Though mine beat faster far than thine,
A hundred months—'twas flow'ry May,
When up the hilly slopes we climbed,
To watch the dying of the day,
And hear the distant church bells chimed.

❀

We loved each other then, Lorena,
More than we ever dared to tell,
And what we might have been, Lorena,

Had but our loving prospered well,
But then, 'tis past, the years are gone,
I'll not call up their shadowy forms,
I'll say to them, "Lost years, sleep on,
Sleep on, nor heed life's pelting storms."

❧

The story of the past, Lorena,
Alas, I care not to repeat,
The hopes that could not last, Lorena,
They lived, but only lived to cheat,
I would not cause e'en one regret,
To rankle in your bosom now,
For "if we try, we may forget,"
Were words of thine long years ago.

❧

Yes, these were words of thine, Lorena,
They burn within my memory yet,
They touch some tender chords, Lorena,
Which thrill and tremble with regret,
'Twas not thy woman's heart that spoke,
Thy heart was always true to me,
A duty, stern and pressing, broke,
The tie which linked my soul to thee.

❧

It matters little now, Lorena,
The past—is in eternal past,

Our heads will soon lie down, Lorena,
Life's tide is ebbing out so fast,
There is a future—Oh, thank God,
Of life this is so small a part,
'Tis dust to dust beneath the sod,
But there, up there, 'tis heart to heart.

Riding a Raid

'Tis old Stonewall, the Rebel, that leans on his sword,
And while we are mounting, prays low to the Lord,
"Now each cavalier that loves Honor and Right,
Let him follow the feather of Stuart tonight."

Chorus:
Come tighten your girth and slacken your rein,
Come buckle your blanket and holster again,
Try the click of your trigger and balance your blade,
For he must ride sure that goes riding a raid!

Now gallop, now gallop, to swim or to ford!
Old Stonewall, still watching, prays low to the Lord,
"Good-bye dear old Rebel! The river's not wide,
And Maryland's lights in her window to guide."

Chorus

There's a man in a white house with blood on his mouth!
If there's Knaves in the North, there are braves in the South,
We are three thousand horses, and not one afraid,
We are three thousand sabres and not a dull blade.

✿

Chorus

✿

Then gallop, then gallop, by ravines and rocks!
Who would bar us the way take his toll in hard knocks,
For with these points of steel, on the line of Penn,
We have made some fine strokes—and we'll make 'em again.

✿

Chorus

Stonewall Jackson's Way

By J. W. Palmer

Come, stack arms, men, pile on the rails,
Stir up the campfire bright,
No matter if the canteen fails,
We'll make a roaring night,
Here Shenandoah brawls along,
Here burly Blue Ridge echoes strong,
To swell the Brigade's rousing song of,
Stonewall Jackson's way.

We see him now, the old slouched hat,
Cocked o'er his eye askew,
The shrewd, dry smile, the speech so pat,
So calm, so blunt, so true,
The "Blue Light Elder" knows 'em well,
Says he, "That's Banks, he's fond of shell,
Lord, save his soul! We'll give him," well,
That's Stonewall Jackson's way.

Silence! Ground arms! Kneel all! Caps off!
Old "Blue Light's" going to pray,
Strangle the fool that dares to scoff!

Attention! It's his way!
Appealing from his native sod,
In *forma pauperis* to God.
"Lay bare Thine arm, stretch forth Thy rod,"
"Amen!" That's Stonewall Jackson's way.

❀

He's in the saddle now! Fall in!
Steady! The whole brigade!
Hill's at the ford, cut off, we'll win,
His way out, ball and blade!
What matter if our shoes are worn?
What matter if our feet are torn?
"Quick-step! We're with him before dawn!"
That's Stonewall Jackson's way.

❀

The sun's bright lances rout the mists,
Of morning, and, by George!
Here's Longstreet struggling in the lists,
Hemmed in an ugly gorge,
Pope and his Yankees, whipped before,
"Bayonets and grape!" Hear Stonewall roar,
"Charge, Stuart! Pay off Ashby's score!"
Is Stonewall Jackson's way.

❀

Ah, maiden, wait and watch, and yearn,
For news of Stonewall's band!

Ah, widow, read, and eyes that burn,
That ring upon thy hand!
Ah, wife, sew on, pray on, hope on!
Thy life shall not be all forlorn,
The foe had better never been born,
That gets in Stonewall's way.

The Bonnie Blue Flag

By Harry McCarthy

We are a band of brothers, and native to the soil,
Fighting for the property we gained by honest toil,
And when our rights were threatened,
The cry rose near and far,
Hurrah for the Bonnie Blue Flag that bears a single star!

Chorus:
Hurrah! Hurrah!
For Southern rights, hurrah!
Hurrah for the Bonnie Blue Flag that bears a single star.

As long as the Union was faithful to her trust,
Like friends and brethren, kind were we, and just,
But now, when Northern treachery attempts our rights to mar,
We hoist on high the Bonnie Blue Flag,
That bears a single star.

Chorus

First gallant South Carolina nobly made the stand,
Then came Alabama and took her by the hand,

Next, quickly, Mississippi, Georgia, and Florida,
All raised on high the Bonnie Blue Flag,
That bears a single star.

✿

Chorus

✿

Ye men of valor gather round the banner of the right,
Texas and fair Louisiana join us in the fight,
Davis, our beloved President, and Stephens, statesmen rare,
Now rally round the Bonnie Blue Flag,
That bears a single star.

✿

Chorus

✿

And here's to brave Virginia, the Old Dominion State,
With the young Confederacy at length has linked her fate,
Impelled by her example, now other States prepare,
To hoist on high the Bonnie Blue Flag,
That bears a single star.

✿

Chorus

✿

Then here's to our Confederacy, strong we are and brave,
Like patriots of old we'll fight, our heritage to save,
And rather than submit to shame, to die we would prefer,
So cheer for the Bonnie Blue Flag that bears a single star.

Chorus

❧

Then cheer, boys, cheer, raise a joyous shout,
For Arkansas and North Carolina now have both gone out,
And let another rousing cheer for Tennessee be given,
The single star of the Bonnie Blue Flag,
Has grown to be eleven.

❧

Chorus

The Rebel Soldier

O Polly, O Polly,
It's for your sake alone,
I've left my old father,
My country and my home,
I've left my old mother,
To weep and to mourn.

❀

Chorus:
I am a Rebel soldier,
And far from my home.

❀

It's grape shot and musket,
And the cannons lumber loud,
There's many a mangled body,
The blanket for their shroud,
There's many a mangled body,
Left on the fields alone.

❀

Chorus

❀

I'll eat when I'm hungry,
I'll drink when I am dry,

If the Yankees don't kill me,
I'll live until I die,
If the Yankees don't kill me,
And cause me to mourn.

❀

Chorus

❀

Here's a good old cup of brandy,
And a glass of nice wine,
You can drink to your true love,
And I will drink to mine,
And you can drink to your true love,
And I'll lament and mourn.

❀

Chorus

❀

I'll build me a castle on the mountain,
On some green mountain high,
Where I can see Polly,
As she is passing by,
Where I can see Polly,
And help her to mourn.

❀

Chorus

The Yellow Rose of Texas

There's a yellow rose in Texas that I am going to see,
No other soldier knows her, no soldier, only me,
She cried so when I left her, it like to broke my heart,
And if I ever find her, we never more will part.

❦

Chorus:
She's the sweetest rose of color this soldier ever knew,
Her eyes are bright as diamonds, they sparkle like the dew,
You may talk about your dearest May and sing of Rosa Lee,
But the Yellow Rose of Texas beats the belles of Tennessee.

❦

Where the Rio Grande is flowing and the starry skies are
bright,
She walks along the river in the quiet summer night,
She thinks if I remember, when we parted long ago,
I promised to come back again and not to leave her so.

❦

Chorus

❦

Oh, now I'm going to find her, for my heart is full of woe,
And we'll sing the song together, that we sung so long ago,
We'll play the banjo gaily, and we'll sing the songs of yore,
And the yellow rose of Texas shall be mine forevermore.

❦

Chorus

We Conquer or Die

By James Pierpont

The war drum is beating, prepare for the fight,
The stern bigot Northman exults in his might,
Gird on your bright weapons your foemen are nigh,
And this be our watchword, "We conquer or die!"
And this be our watchword, "We conquer or die!"

❀

The trumpet is sounding from mountain to shore,
Your swords and your lances must slumber no more,
Fling forth to the sunlight your banner on high,
Inscribed with the watchword, "We conquer or die!"
Inscribed with the watchword, "We conquer or die!"

❀

March on to the battlefield, there to do or dare,
With shoulder to shoulder all danger to share,
And let your proud watchword ring up to the sky,
Till the blue arch re-echoes, "We conquer or die!"
Till the blue arch re-echoes, "We conquer or die!"

❀

Press forward undaunted, nor think of retreat,
The enemy's host on the threshold to meet,
Strike firm, till the foeman before you shall fly,
Appalled by the watchword, "We conquer or die!"
Appalled by the watchword, "We conquer or die!"

Go forth in the pathway our forefathers trod,
We too fight for Freedom, our Captain is God,
Their blood in our veins, with their honors we vie,
Their's too, was the watchword, "We conquer or die!"
Their's too, was the watchword, "We conquer or die!"

We strike for the South-Mountain, Valley, and Plain,
For the South we will conquer, again and again,
Her day of salvation and triumph is nigh,
Our's then be the watchword, "We conquer or die!"
Our's then be the watchword, "We conquer or die!"

Aura Lea

By W.W. Fosdick

When the blackbird in the spring, on the willow tree,
Sat and rocked, I heard him sing, singing Aura Lea,
Aura Lea, Aura Lea, maid of golden hair,
Sunshine came along with thee, and swallows in the air.

❀

Chorus:
Aura Lea, Aura Lea, maid of golden hair,
Sunshine came along with thee, and swallows in the air.

❀

In thy blush the rose was born, music when you spake,
Through thine azure eye the morn, sparkling seemed to break,
Aura Lea, Aura Lea, bird of crimson wing,
Never song have sung to me, in that sweet spring.

❀

Chorus

❀

Aura Lea! The bird may flee, the willows golden hair,
Swing through winter fitfully, on the stormy air,
Yet if thy blue eyes I see, gloom will soon depart,
For to me, sweet Aura Lea is sunshine through the heart.

Chorus

When the mistletoe was green, midst the winter's snows,
Sunshine in thy face was seen, kissing lips of rose,
Aura Lea, Aura Lea, take my golden ring,
Love and light return with thee, and swallows with the spring.

Pat Murphy of the
Irish Brigade

Says Pat to his mother, "It looks strange to see,
Brothers fighting in such a queer manner,
But I'll fight till I die if I never get killed for,
America's bright starry banner."

Chorus:
Faraway in the East was a dashing young blade,
And the song he was singin' so gaily,
'Twas honest Pat Murphy of the Irish Brigade,
And the song of the splintered shillelagh.

The morning soon broke and poor Paddy awoke,
He found Rebels to give satisfaction,
And the drummers were beating the Devil's sad tune,
They were calling the boys into action.

Chorus

Sure, the day after the battle, the dead lay in heaps,
And Pat Murphy lay bleeding and gory,

With a hole through his head by some enemy's ball,
That ended his passion for glory.

❀

Chorus

❀

No more in the camp will his letters be read,
Or his song be heard singing so gaily,
But he died far away from the friends that he loved,
And far from the land of shillelagh.

❀

Chorus

Tenting Tonight on the Old Campground

By Walter Kittredge

We're tenting tonight on the old campground,
Give us a song to cheer,
Our weary hearts, a song of home,
And friend we love so dear.

Chorus:
Many are the hearts that are weary tonight,
Wishing for the war to cease,
Many are the hearts that are looking for the right,
To see the dawn of peace,
Tenting tonight, tenting tonight,
Tenting on the old campground.

We've been tenting tonight on the old campground,
Thinking of days gone by,
Of the loved ones at home that gave us the hand,
And the tear that said "Goodbye!"

❀

❀

We are tired of war on the old campground,
Many are dead and gone,
Of the brave and true who've left their homes,
Others been wounded long.

❀

Chorus

❀

We've been fighting today on the old campground,
Many are lying near,
Some are dead and some are dying,
Many are in tears.

❀

Chorus

❀

Many are the heart who are weary tonight,
Wishing for the war to cease,
Many are the hearts that are looking for the right,
To see the dawn of peace,
Dying tonight, dying tonight,
Dying on the old campground.

When Johnny Comes Marching Home

By Patrick S. Gilmore

❦

When Johnny comes marching home again,
Hurrah! Hurrah!
We'll give him a hearty welcome then,
Hurrah! Hurrah!
The men will cheer, the boys will shout,
The ladies, they will all turn out,
And we'll all feel gay when Johnny comes marching home.

❦

The old church bell will peal with joy,
Hurrah! Hurrah!
To welcome home our darling boy,
Hurrah! Hurrah!
The village lads and lassies say,
With roses they will strew the way,
And we'll all feel gay when Johnny comes marching home.

❦

Get ready for the Jubilee,
Hurrah! Hurrah!
We'll give the hero three times three,

Hurrah! Hurrah!
The laurel wreath is ready now,
To place upon his loyal brow,
And we'll all feel gay when Johnny comes marching home.

❦

Let love and friendship on that day,
Hurrah! Hurrah!
Their choicest treasures then display,
Hurrah! Hurrah!
And let each one perform some part,
To fill with joy the warrior's heart,
And we'll all feel gay when Johnny comes marching home.

CHAPTER

7

FAVORITES FROM THE TURN
OF THE CENTURY

IN THE LATE nineteenth century, a short stretch of West 28th Street in Manhattan earned the name "Tin Pan Alley" for the round-the-clock clatter that emanated from the offices of music publishers on that block. Day and night, hopeful songwriters banged away on their typewriters, hoping to write a hit for the ever-expanding sheet music market.

No one knows just how many songs were written in Tin Pan Alley's heyday, but many are still popular today. From the turn of the century to the beginning of the Roaring Twenties, countless of these "standards" were written. Love songs were timeless and always popular, but so were songs that celebrated uniquely American experiences, such as "Take Me Out to the Ball Game" (page 395), "Give My Regards to Broadway" (page 341), and "Meet Me in St. Louis," which sang of the 1903 St. Louis World's Fair.

Many of the songs in this chapter are from World War I, such as "Keep the Home Fires Burning" (page 415) and "Over There" (page 419). The most enduring song of World War I had nothing to do with war, however. "It's a Long Way to Tipperary" is a comic song about an Irishman pining for his homeland, but the theme of homesickness struck the right note with English and American soldiers alike, and they sang it on marches throughout the war, sometimes with lyrics of their own invention, such as "That's the wrong way to tickle Mary!"

After The Ball

By Charles K. Harris

A little maiden climbed an old man's knees,
Begged for a story, "Do uncle, please!
Why are you single, why live alone?
Have you no babies, have you no home?"
"I had a sweetheart, years, years ago,
Where she is now, pet, you will soon know,
List to the story, I'll tell it all,
I believed her faithless after the ball."

Chorus:
After the ball is over, after the break of morn,
After the dancers' leaving, after the stars are gone,
Many a heart is aching, if you could read them all,
Many the hopes that have vanished after the ball.

"Bright lights were flashing in the grand ballroom,
Softly the music playing sweet tunes,
There came my sweetheart, my love, my own,
"I wish some water, leave me alone."
When I returned, dear, there stood a man,
Kissing my sweetheart as lovers can,

Down fell the glass, pet, broken, that's all,
  Just as my heart was after the ball."

❀

Chorus

❀

"Long years have passed, child, I have never wed,
  True to my lost love though she is dead,
  She tried to tell me, tried to explain,
  I would not listen, pleadings were vain,
  One day a letter came from that man,
  He was her brother, the letter ran,
  That's why I'm lonely, no home at all,
  I broke her heart, pet, after the ball."

❀

Chorus

And The Band Played On
(Casey Would Waltz
with the Strawberry Blonde)

By Charles B. Ward and John E. Palmer

Casey would waltz,
With the strawberry blonde,
And the band played on,
He'd glide 'cross the floor,
With the girl he'd adore,
And the band played on,
But his brain was so loaded,
It nearly exploded,
The poor girl,
Would shake with alarm,
He'd never leave the girl,
With the strawberry curl,
And the band played on.

Bird in a Gilded Cage

By Arthur J. Lamb and Harry Von Tilzer

The ballroom was filled with fashion's throng,
It shone with a thousand lights,
And there was a woman who passed along,
The fairest of all the sights,
A girl to her lover then softly sighed,
"There's riches at her command."
"But she married for wealth, not for love," he cried!
"Though she lives in a mansion grand."

❀

Chorus:
"She's only a bird in a gilded cage,
A beautiful sight to see,
You may think she's happy and free from care,
She's not, though she seems to be,
'Tis sad when you think of her wasted life,
For youth cannot mate with age,
And her beauty was sold for an old man's gold,
She's a bird in a gilded cage."

❀

I stood in a churchyard just at eve,
When sunset adorned the west,

And looked at the people who'd come to grieve,
For loved ones now laid at rest,
A tall marble monument marked the grave,
Of one who'd been fashion's queen,
And I thought, "She is happier here at rest,
Than to have people say when seen."

❀

Chorus

DOWN WENT MCGINTY

By Joseph Flynn

Sunday morning just at nine,
Dan McGinty dressed so fine,
Stood looking at a very high stone wall,
When his friend, young Pat McCann, says, "I'll bet five
dollars, Dan, I could carry you to the top without a fall."
So on his shoulders he took Dan,
To climb the ladder he began,
And soon commenced to reach up near the top,
When McGinty, cute old rogue,
To win the five he did let go,
Never thinking just how far he'd have to drop.

❀

Down went McGinty to the bottom of the wall,
And tho' he won the five, he was more dead than alive,
Sure his ribs and nose and back were broke from,
Getting such a fall,
Dressed in his best suit of clothes.

❀

From the hospital Mac went home,
When they fixed his broken bones,

To find he was the father of a child,
So to celebrate it right, his friends he went to invite,
And soon he was drinking whiskey fast and wild,
Then he waddled down the street in his Sunday suit so neat,
Holding up his head as proud as John the Great,
But in the sidewalk was a hole, to receive a ton of coal,
That McGinty never saw till just too late.

❧

Down went McGinty to the bottom of the hole,
Then the driver of the cart gave the load of coal a start,
And it took us half an hour to dig,
McGinty from the coal,
Dresse'd in his best suit of clothes.

❧

Now McGinty raved and swore,
About his clothes he felt so sore,
And an oath he took he'd kill the man or die,
So he tightly grabbed his stick and hit the driver a lick,
Then he raised a little shanty on his eye,
But two policemen saw the muss and they,
Soon joined in the fuss,
Then they ran McGinty in for being drunk,
And the Judge says with a smile,
We will keep you for a while,
In a cell to sleep upon a prison bunk.

❧

Down went McGinty to the bottom of the jail,
Where his board would cost him nix,
And he stay'd exactly six,
They were big long months he stopp'd for,
No one went his bail,
Dressed in his best suit of clothes.

❀

Now McGinty thin and pale one,
Fine day got out of jail,
And with joy to see his boy was nearly wild,
To his house he quickly ran to see his wife Bedaley Ann,
But she skipp'd away and took along the child,
Then he gave up in despair and,
He madly pulled his hair,
As he stood one day upon the river shore,
Knowing well he couldn't swim,
He did foolishly jump in,
Although watch he had never took before.

❀

Down went McGinty to the bottom of the sea,
And he must be very wet for they,
Haven't found him yet,
But they say his ghost comes round the docks before
The break of day,
Dressed in his best suit of clothes.

Give My Regards to Broadway

By George M. Cohan

At a port in France one morning,
Waiting for my ship to sail,
Yankee soldiers on a furlough,
Came to get the latest mail,
I told them I was on my way,
To old Manhattan Isle,
They all gathered about,
As the vessel pulled out,
And said, with a smile.

❁

Chorus:
Give my regards to Broadway,
Remember me to Herald Square,
Tell all the gang at Forty-Second Street,
That I will soon be there,
Whisper of how I'm yearning,
To mingle with the old time throng,
Give my regards to old Broadway,
And say that I'll be there e'er long.

❁

Say hello to dear old Coney Isle,
If there you chance to be,
When you're at the Waldorf have a smile,
And charge it up to me,
Mention my name ev'ry place you go,
As 'round the town you roam,
Wish you'd call on my gal,
Now remember, old pal,
When you get back home.

❧

Chorus

Hello My Baby

By Ida Emerson and Joseph E. Howard

Hello, my baby,
Hello, my honey,
Hello, my ragtime gal.

❀

Send me a kiss by wire,
Baby, my heart's on fire.

❀

If you refuse me,
Honey, you'll lose me,
Then you'll be left alone.

❀

Oh baby, telephone,
And tell me I'm your own.

❀

Hello, my baby,
Hello, my honey,
Hello, my ragtime gal.

❀

Send me a kiss by wire,
Baby, my heart's on fire.

❀

If you refuse me,
Honey, you'll lose me,
Then you'll be left alone.

❀

Oh baby, telephone,
And tell me I'm your own.

Turn Off Your Light Mr. Moon Man

By Nora Bayes and Jack Norworth

When the Moon is shining yellow,
And a girl is with her fellow,
Both are getting nice and mellow,
In the bright moonlight.

❦

If the Moon-Man should discover,
Sweethearts meeting under cover,
Can you blame that girl and lover,
If they say "Turn off that light!"

❦

Chorus:
Turn off your light, Mr. Moon-Man!
Go and hide your face behind the clouds,
Can't you see that couples wanna spoon, and,
Two is company and three's a crowd.

❦

When each little lad and lady,
Find a spot so nice and shady,
That's your cue to say "Goodnight, goodnight!"
And if they want to spoon,

Listen Mr. Moon,
Be a sport and turn off your light.

❀

All the lads and little misses,
Who are fond of hugs and kisses,
Must remember half the bliss,
Is found on any cloudy night.

❀

Nighttime is the time for spooning,
Serenades and lovers crooning,
Preliminary honeymooning,
Calls for darkness, not for light!

❀

Chorus

❀

When each little lad and lady,
Find a spot so nice and shady,
That's your cue to say "Goodnight, goodnight!"
And if they want to spoon,
Listen Mr. Moon,
Be a sport and turn off your light.

I Don't Want to Play In Your Yard

By Philip Wingate

Once there lived side by side, two little maids,
Used to dress just alike, hair down in braids,
Blue ging'am pinafores, stockings of red,
Little sun bonnets tied on each pretty head.

Chorus:
I don't want to play in your yard,
I don't like you anymore,
You'll be sorry when you see me,
Sliding down our cellar door,
You can't holler down our rain barrel,
You can't climb our apple tree,
I don't want to play in your yard,
If you won't be good to me.

When school was over secrets they'd tell,
Whispering arm in arm, down by the well,
One day a quarrel came, hot tears were shed,
"You can't play in our yard," but the other said:

❀

Chorus

❀

Next day two little maids each other miss,
Quarrels are soon made up, sealed with a kiss,
Then hand in hand again, happy they go,
Friends all through life to be, they love each other so.

❀

Chorus

❀

Soon school days pass away, sorrows and bliss,
But love remembers yet, quarrels and kiss,
In sweet dreams of childhood, we hear the cry,
"You can't play in our yard," and the old reply:

❀

Chorus

I Love You Truly

By Carrie Jacobs-Bond

I love you truly, truly dear,
Life with its sorrow, life with its tear,
Fades into dreams when I feel you are near,
For I love you truly, truly dear!

A love 'tis something, to feel your kind hand,
Ah yes, 'tis something, by your side to stand,
Gone is the sorrow, gone doubt and fear,
For you love me truly, truly dear!

There's a Time Each Year
(In the Good Old Summertime)

By George Evans and Ren Shields

There's a time each year,
That we always hold dear,
Good old summertime,
With the birds and the trees'es,
And sweet scented breezes,
Good old summertime,
When your day's work is over,
Then you are in clover,
And life is one beautiful rhyme,
No trouble annoying,
Each one is enjoying,
The good old summertime.

❦

Chorus:
In the good old summertime,
In the good old summertime,
Strolling through a shady lane,
With your baby mine,
You hold her hand and she holds yours,
And that's a very good sign,

That she's your tootsie wootsie,
In the good old summertime.

❀

To swim in the pool,
You play "hooky" from school,
Good old summertime,
You play "ring-a rosie,"
With Jim, Kate and Josie,
Good old summertime,
Those days full of pleasure,
We now fondly treasure,
When we never thought it a crime,
To be stealing cherries,
With faces brown as berries,
In the good old summertime.

❀

Chorus

MEET ME IN ST. LOUIS, LOUIS

By Andrew B. Sterling and Frederick Allen "Kerry" Mills

When Louis came home to the flat,
He hung up his coat and his hat,
He gazed all around, but no wifey he found,
So he said "where can Flossie be at?"
A note on the table he spied,
He read it just once, then he cried,
It ran, "Louis dear, it's too slow for me here,
So I think I will go for a ride."

❀

Chorus:
"Meet me in St. Louis, Louis,
Meet me at the fair,
Don't tell me the lights are shining,
Any place but there,
We will dance the Hoochee Koochee,
I will be your tootsie wootsie,
If you will meet me in St. Louis, Louis,
Meet me at the fair."

❀

The dresses that hung in the hall,
Were gone, she had taken them all,

She took all his rings and the rest of his things,
The picture he missed from the wall,
"What! Moving!" The janitor said,
"Your rent is paid three months ahead."
"What good is the flat?" said poor Louis, "Read that."
And the janitor smiled as he read.

❧

Chorus

My Wild Irish Rose

By Chauncey Olcott

If you'll listen, I'll sing you a sweet little song,
Of a flower that's now drooped and dead,
Yet dearer to me, yes, than all of its mates,
Though each holds aloft its proud head,
'Twas given to me by a girl that I know,
Since we've met, faith, I've known no repose,
She is dearer by far than the world's brightest star,
And I call her my wild Irish Rose.

Chorus:
My wild Irish Rose,
The sweetest flower that grows,
You may search everywhere,
But none can compare,
With my wild Irish Rose,
My wild Irish Rose,
The dearest flower that grows,
And some day for my sake,
She may let me take,
The bloom from my wild Irish Rose.

They may sing of their roses which, by other names,
Would smell just as sweetly, they say,
But I know that my Rose would never consent,
To have that sweet name taken away,
Her glances are shy when ever I pass by,
The bower, where my true love grows,
And my one wish has been that some day I may win,
The heart of my wild Irish Rose.

❀

Chorus

Rock-A-Bye Baby

Rock-a-bye, baby,
In the treetop,
When the wind blows,
The cradle will rock,
When the bough breaks,
The cradle will fall,
And down will come baby,
Cradle and all.

❀

Baby is drowsing,
Cozy and fair,
Mother sits near,
In her rocking chair,
Forward and back,
The cradle she swings,
And though baby sleeps,
He hears what she sings.

❀

From the high rooftops,
Down to the sea,
No one's as dear,
As baby to me,
Wee little fingers,

Eyes wide and bright,
Now sound asleep,
Until morning light.

Sweet Rosie O'Grady

By Maude Nugent and William Jerome

Down around the corner,
Of the street where I reside,
There lives the cutest little girl,
That I have ever spied,
Her name is Rose O'Grady,
And I don't mind telling you,
That she's the sweetest little rose,
This garden ever grew.

Chorus:
Sweet Rosie O'Grady,
My dear little Rose,
She's my steady lady,
Most everyone knows,
And when we are married,
How happy we'll be,
I love Sweet Rosie O'Grady and,
Rosie O'Grady loves me.

I never shall forget the day,
She promised to be mine,

As we sat telling love-tales,
In the golden summertime,
It was on her finger then,
I placed a small engagement ring,
While in the trees, the little birds,
This song they seemed to sing.

❀

Chorus

You're a Grand Old Flag

By George M. Cohan

Chorus:
You're a grand old flag,
You're a high-flying flag,
And forever in peace may you wave,
You're the emblem of the land I love,
The home of the free and the brave,
Ev'ry heart beats true,
'Neath the Red, White and Blue,
Where there's never a boast or a brag,
But should auld acquaintance be forgot,
Keep your eyes on the grand old flag!

There's a feeling comes a-stealing,
And it sets my brain a-reeling,
When I'm listening to the music of a military band,
Any tune like "Yankee Doodle,"
Simply sets me off my noodle,
It's that patriotic something that no one can understand.

"Way down South, in the land of cotton,"
Melody untiring,
Ain't that inspiring?
Hurrah! Hurrah! We'll join the Jubilee!
And that's going some,

For the Yankees, by gum!
Red, white and blue, I am for you!
Honest, you're a grand old flag!

※

Chorus

※

I'm a cranky hanky panky,
I'm a dead square, honest Yankee,
And I'm mighty proud of that old flag,
That flies for Uncle Sam.

※

Though I don't believe in raving,
Ev'ry time I see it waving,
There's a chill runs up my back that,
Makes me glad I'm what I am.

※

Here's a land with a million soldiers,
That's if we should need 'em,
We'll fight for freedom!

※

Hurrah! Hurrah! For every Yankee tar,
And old G.A.R.,
Ev'ry stripe, ev'ry star,
Red, white and blue,
Hats off to you,
Honest, you're a grand old flag!

※

Chorus

Sweet Adeline (The Flower Song)

In the evening when I sit alone a-dreaming,
Of days gone by, love, to me so dear,
There's a picture that in fancy oft' appearing,
Brings back the time, love, when you were near,
It is then I wonder where you are, my darling,
And if your heart to me is still the same,
For the sighing wind and nightingale a-singing,
Are breathing only your own sweet name.

❁

Chorus:
Sweet Adeline, (My Adeline),
My Adeline, (My Adeline),
At night, dear heart, (At night, dear heart),
For you I pine, (For you I pine),
In all my dreams, (In all my dreams),
Your fair face beams, (Your fair face beams),
You're the flower of my heart,
Sweet Adeline, (My Adeline).

❁

I can see your smiling face as when we wandered,
Down by the brook-side, just you and I,
And it seems so real at times 'til I awaken,
To find all vanished, a dream gone by,

If we must meet sometime in after years, my darling,
I trust that I will find your love still mine,
Though my heart is sad and clouds above are hov'ring,
The sun again, love, for me would shine.

❀

Chorus

America The Beautiful

By Katharine Lee Bates

O beautiful for spacious skies,
For amber waves of grain,
For purple mountain majesties,
Above the fruited plain!
America! America!
God shed his grace on thee,
And crown thy good with brotherhood,
From sea to shining sea!

❀

O beautiful for pilgrim feet,
Whose stern, impassioned stress,
A thoroughfare for freedom beat,
Across the wilderness!

❀

America! America!
God mend thine every flaw,
Confirm thy soul in self-control,
Thy liberty in law!

❀

O beautiful for heroes proved in liberating strife,
Who more than self the country loved,

And mercy more than life!
America! America!
May God thy gold refine,
Till all success be nobleness,
And every gain divine!

❀

O beautiful for patriot dreams,
That sees beyond the years,
Thine alabaster cities gleam,
Undimmed by human tears!
America! America!
God shed his grace on thee,
And crown thy good with brotherhood,
From sea to shining sea!

❀

O beautiful for halcyon skies,
For amber waves of grain,
For purple mountain majesties,
Above the enameled plain!
America! America!
God shed his grace on thee,
Till souls wax fair as earth and air,
And music-hearted sea!

❀

O beautiful for pilgrims feet,
Whose stern impassioned stress,

A thoroughfare for freedom beat,
Across the wilderness!
America! America!
God shed his grace on thee,
Till paths be wrought through,
Wilds of thought,
By pilgrim foot and knee!

※

O beautiful for glory-tale,
Of liberating strife,
When once and twice,
For man's avail,
Men lavished precious life!
America! America!
God shed his grace on thee,
Till selfish gain no longer stain,
The banner of the free!

※

O beautiful for patriot dreams,
That sees beyond the years,
Thine alabaster cities gleam,
Undimmed by human tears!
America! America!
God shed his grace on thee,
Till nobler men keep once again,
Thy whiter jubilee!

Buffalo Gals

As I was walking down the street,
Down the street, down the street,
A pretty gal I chance to meet,
Under the silvery moon.

Chorus:
Buffalo gals, won't you come out tonight?
Come out tonight, Come out tonight?
Buffalo gals, won't you come out tonight,
And dance by the light of the moon.

I asked her if she'd stop and talk,
Stop and talk, Stop and talk,
Her feet covered up the whole sidewalk,
She was fair to view.

Chorus

I asked her if she'd be my wife,
Be my wife, be my wife,
Then I'd be happy all my life,
If she'd marry me.

Chorus

GO DOWN, MOSES

When Israel was in Egypt's land,
Let my people go!
Oppressed so hard they could not stand,
Let my people go!

Chorus:
Go down, Moses,
Way down in Egypt's land,
Tell old Pharaoh,
To let my people go!

"Thus said the Lord," bold Moses said,
Let my people go!
"If not I'll smite your first born dead."
Let my people go!

Chorus

No more shall they in bondage toil,
Let my people go!
Let them come out with Egypt's spoil,
Let my people go!

❀

Chorus

❀

Oh, let us all from bondage flee,
Let my people go!
And let us all in Christ be free,
Let my people go!

❀

Chorus

❀

You need not always weep and mourn,
Let my people go!
And wear these slav'ry chains forlorn,
Let my people go!

❀

Chorus

❀

Your foes shall not before you stand,
Let my people go!
And you'll possess fair Canaan's land,
Let my people go!

❀

Chorus

He's Got the Whole World in His Hand

He's got the whole world in his hand,
He's got the whole world in his hand,
The whole wide world in His hand,
He's got the whole world in his hand,
He's got the whole world in his hand.

He's got you and me brother, in his hand, *(Repeat three times)*
He's got the whole world in his hand.

He's got the little bitty babies in his hand, *(Repeat three times)*
He's got the whole world in his hand.

He's got the lyin' man in his hand, *(Repeat three times)*
He's got the whole world in his hand.

He's got the gamblin' man in his hand, *(Repeat three times)*
He's got the whole world in his hand.

The Man on the Flying Trapeze

By George Leybourne

Once I was happy, but now I'm forlorn,
Like an old coat that is tattered and torn,
Left on this world to fret and to mourn,
Betrayed by a maid in her teens.

The girl that I loved she was handsome,
I tried all I knew her to please,
But I could not please her one quarter so well,
As the man upon the trapeze.

Chorus:
He'd fly through the air with the greatest of ease,
That daring young man on the flying trapeze,
His movements were graceful, all girls he could please,
And my love he purloined away.

This young man by name was Signor Bona Slang,
Tall, big and handsome, as well made as Chang,
Where'er he appeared the hall loudly rang,
With ovation from all people there.

He'd smile from the bar on the people below,
And one night he smiled on my love,
She wink'd back at him and she shouted "Bravo,"
As he hung by his nose up above.

❧

Chorus

❧

Her father and mother were both on my side,
And very hard tried to make her my bride,
Her father he sighed, and her mother she cried,
To see her throw herself away,
'Twas all no avail, she went there every night,
And would throw him bouquets on the stage,
Which caused him to meet her, how he ran me down,
To tell you would take a whole page.

❧

Chorus

❧

One night I as usual went to her dear home,
Found there her father and mother alone,
I asked for my love, and soon they made known,
To my horror that she'd run away.

Chorus

She'd packed up her box and eloped in the night,
With him, with the greatest of ease,
From two stories high he had lowered her down,
To the ground on his flying trapeze.

Chorus

Some months after this I went to the hall,
Was greatly surprised to see on the wall,
A bill in red letters, which did my heart gall,
That she was appearing with him.

Chorus

He'd taught her gymnastics and dressed her in tights,
To help him live at his ease,
And made her assume a masculine name,
And now she goes on the trapeze.

She'd fly through the air with the greatest of ease,
You'd think her the man young man on the flying trapeze,
Her movements were graceful, all girls she could please,
And that was the end of my love.

On Top of Old Smokey

On top of Old Smokey,
All covered with snow,
I lost my true lover,
For courting too slow.

※

Now, courting is a pleasure,
And parting is grief,
And a false-hearted lover,
Is worse than a thief.

※

A thief will just rob you,
And take what you have,
But a false-hearted lover,
Will lead you to the grave.

※

And the grave will decay you,
And turn you to dust,
Not one girl in a hundred,
A poor boy can trust.

※

They'll hug you and kiss you,
And tell you more lies,

Than the crossties on the railroad,
Or stars in the sky.

&

So, come all you young maidens,
And listen to me,
Never place your affection,
On a green willow tree.

&

For the leaves they will wither,
And the roots they will die,
You'll all be forsaken,
And never know why.

&

On top of Old Smokey,
All covered with snow,
I lost my true lover,
For courting too slow.

While Strolling Through the Park

While strolling through the park one day,
All in the merry month of May,
A roguish pair of eyes, they took me by surprise,
In a moment my poor heart they stole away,
O a sunny smile was all she gave to me,
And of course we were as happy as could be,
So neatly I raised my hat,
And made a polite remark,
I never shall forget that lovely afternoon,
When I met her at the fountain in the park.

I'm Always Chasing Rainbows

By Joseph McCarthy and Harry Carroll

Chorus:
I'm always chasing rainbows,
Watching clouds drifting by,
My dreams are just like all my schemes,
Ending in the sky.

❀

Some fellas search and find the sunshine,
I always look and find the rain,
Some fellas make a winning sometime,
I never even make a gain,
Believe me.

❀

I'm always chasing rainbows,
Waiting to find a little bluebird in vain.

❀

Chorus

❀

Some fellas search and find the sunshine,
I always look and find the rain,
Some fellas make a winning sometime,

I never even make a gain,
Believe me.

❧

I'm always chasing rainbows,
Waiting to find a little bluebird in vain.

I'm Forever Blowing Bubbles

By Albert C. Campbell and Henry Burr

I'm dreaming dreams,
I'm scheming schemes,
I'm building castles high,
They're born anew,
Their days are few,
Just like a sweet butterfly,
And as the daylight is dawning,
They come again in the morning.

Chorus:
I'm forever blowing bubbles,
Pretty bubbles in the air,
They fly so high,
Nearly reach the sky,
Then like my dreams,
They fade and die,
Fortune's always hiding,
I've looked everywhere,
I'm forever blowing bubbles,
Pretty bubbles in the air.

A Pretty Girl Is Like a Melody

By Irving Berlin

I have an ear for music,
And I have an eye for a maid,
I like a pretty girlie,
With each pretty tune that's played,
They go together,
Like sunny weather goes with the month of May,
I've studied girls and music,
So I'm qualified to say.

Chorus:
A pretty girl is like a melody,
That haunts you night and day,
Just like the strain of a haunting refrain,
She'll start up-on a marathon,
And run around your brain,
You can't escape she's in your memory,
By morning night and noon,
She will leave you and then come back again,
A pretty girl is just like a pretty tune.

Rock-A-Bye Your Baby With a Dixie Melody

By Jean Schwartz, Sam Lewis, and Joe Young

Mammy mine, your little rolling stone,
That rolled away, rolled away,
Mammy mine, your rolling stone is,
Rolling home today, there to stay!
I want to see your smiling face, smile a welcome smile,
I want to feel your fond embrace, listen, mammy mine!

Chorus:
Rock-a-bye your baby with a Dixie melody,
When you croon, croon a little tune from the heart,
Of Dixie!
Just hang that cradle, mammy mine,
On the Mason-Dixon line, And swing it from Virginia,
To Tennessee with all the pull that's in ya.

"Weep No More, My Lady," sing that song again for me,
And "Old Black Joe," just as though you had me on,
Your knee!
A million baby kisses I'll deliver,
If you will only sing that "Swanee River,"

Rock-a-bye your rock-a-bye baby with that,
Dixie melody.

❀

Chorus

❀

Ah, they're playing "Weep No More, My Lady!"
Mammy, sing it again for me,
And "Old Black Joe," just as though you had me on,
Your knee!
A million baby kisses—I'll deliver,
If you will, oh please sing the "Swanee River,"
Rock-a-bye your rock-a-bye baby with that,
Dixie melody.

Till We Meet Again (God Be with You)

By William G. Tomer

God be with you till we meet again,
By His counsels guide, uphold you,
With His sheep securely fold you,
God be with you till we meet again.

Chorus:
Till we meet, till we meet,
Till we meet at Jesus' feet,
Till we meet, till we meet,
God be with you till we meet again.

God be with you till we meet again,
'Neath His wings securely hide you,
Daily manna still provide you,
God be with you till we meet again.

Chorus

God be with you till we meet again,
When life's perils thick confound you,

Put His arms unfailing round you,
God be with you till we meet again.

❀

Chorus

❀

God be with you till we meet again,
Keep love's banner floating over you,
Smite death's threat'ning wave before you,
God be with you till we meet again.

❀

Chorus

Ah! Sweet Mystery of Life

By Rida Johnson Young

Ah! Sweet mystery of life, at last I've found thee,
Ah! I know at last the secret of it all,
All the longing, striving, seeking, waiting, yearning,
The burning hopes, the joys and idle tears that fall!

For 'tis love, and love alone, the world is seeking,
And it's love, and love alone, that can reply,
'Tis the answer, 'tis the end and all of living,
For it is love alone that rules for aye!

Alexander's Ragtime Band

By Irving Berlin

Oh, ma honey, oh, ma honey, better hurry and let's meander,
Ain't you goin'? Ain't you goin'?
To the leader-man, ragged meter man?
Oh, ma honey, oh, ma honey, let me take you to Alexander's,
Grand stand brass band, ain't you comin' along?

❀

Chorus:
Come on and hear! Come on and hear!
Alexander's rag-time band!
Come on and hear! Come on and hear!
It's the best band in the land!
They can play a bugle call like you never heard be-fore,
So natural that you want to go to war,
That's just the bestest band what am, oh, ma honey lamb,
Come on a-long, come on along, let me take you by the hand,
Up to the man, the funny man, who's the leader of the band,
And if you care to hear the Swanee River played in rag-time,
Come on and hear, come on and hear,
Alexander's Rag-Time Band.

❀

Oh, ma honey, oh, ma honey,
There's a fiddle with notes that screeches,
Like a chicken, like a chicken,
And the clarinet is a colored pet,
Come and listen, come and listen,
To a classical band what's peaches,
Come now, some-how, better hurry along!

❧

Chorus

By the Light of the Silvery Moon

By Edward Madden and Gus Edwards

Place: park, scene: dark,
Silvery moon is shining through the trees,
Cast two, me, you, sound of kisses floating on the breeze,
Act one, begun. Dialogue, "Where would you like to spoon?"
My cue, with you, underneath the silvery moon.

✿

By the light of the silvery moon,
I want to spoon, to my honey I'll croon love's tune,
Honeymoon keep a shining in June,
Your silvery beams will bring love dreams,
We'll be cuddling soon,
By the silvery moon.

✿

Act two, scene new: roses blooming all around the place,
Cast three: you, me,
Preacher with a solemn looking face,
Choir sings, bell rings,
Preacher, "You are wed for evermore."
Act two, all through, every night the same encore.

✿

By the light, (By the light, By the light),
Of the silvery moon, (The silvery moon),
I want to spoon, (Want to spoon, Want to spoon),
To my honey I'll croon love's tune,
Honeymoon, (Honeymoon, Honeymoon),
Keep a shining in June, (Keep a shining in June),
Your silvery beams will bring love dreams,
We'll be cuddling soon,
By the silvery moon.

❀

Your silvery beams will bring love dreams,
We'll be cuddling soon,
By the silvery moon, (The silvery moon),
By the light that's silvery!

I Want a Girl (Just Like the Girl)

By Harry Von Tilzer and William Dillon

When I was a boy my mother often said to me,
Get married boy and see,
How happy you will be,
I have looked all over, but no girlie can I find,
Who seems to be just like the little girl I have in mind,
I will have to look around,
Until the right one I have found.

❀

Chorus:
I want a girl,
Just like the girl who married dear old Dad,
She was a pearl,
And the only girl that Daddy ever had,
A real old fashioned girl with heart so true,
One who loves nobody else but you,
Oh I want a girl,
Just like the girl that married dear old Dad.

❀

By the old mill stream there sits a couple old and gray,
Though years have rolled away,
Their hearts are young today,

Mother dear looks up at Dad,
With love light in her eye,
He steals a kiss, a fond embrace,
While evening breezes sigh,
They're as happy as can be,
So that's the kind of love for me.

Chorus

I Wonder Who's Kissing Her Now

By Will M. Hough, Frank R. Adams,
Harold Orlob, and Joe Howard

You have loved lots of girls in the sweet long-ago,
And each has meant heaven to you,
You have vowed your affection to each one in turn,
And have sworn to them all you'd be true,
You have kissed 'neath the moon while,
The world seemed in tune,
Then you've left her to hunt a new game,
Does it ever occur to you later my boy,
That she's prob'ly doing the same?

Chorus:
I wonder who's kissing her now,
I wonder who's teaching her how,
I wonder who's looking into her eyes,
Breathing sighs, telling lies,
I wonder who's buying the wine for lips,
That I used to call mine,
I wonder if she ever tells him of me,
I wonder who's kissing her now.

If you want to feel wretched and lonely and blue,
Just imagine the girl you love best,
In the arms of some fellow who's stealing a kiss,
From the lips that you once fondly pressed,
But the world moves apace and the loves of today,
Flit away with a smile and a tear,
So you can never tell who's kissing her now,
Or just whom you'll be kissing next year.

Chorus

LET ME CALL YOU SWEETHEART

By Beth Slater Whitson and Leo Friedman

I am dreaming Dear of you, day by day,
Dreaming when the skies are blue, when they're gray,
When the silv'ry moonlight gleams,
Still I wander on in dreams,
In a land of love, it seems,
Just with you.

❀

Chorus:
Let me call you "Sweetheart," I'm in love with you,
Let me hear you whisper that you love me too,
Keep the love-light glowing in your eyes so true,
Let me call you "Sweetheart," I'm in love with you.

❀

Longing for you all the while,
More and more,
Longing for the sunny smile, I adore,
Birds are singing far and near,
Roses blooming ev'rywhere,
You, alone, my heart can cheer, you, just you.

❀

Chorus

TAKE ME OUT TO THE BALL GAME

By Jack Norworth

Katie Casey was baseball mad,
Had the fever and had it bad,
Just to root for the home town crew,
Ev'ry sou Katie blew,
On a Saturday, her young beau,
Called to see if she'd like to go,
To see a show but Miss Kate said,
"No, I'll tell you what you can do."

Chorus:
"Take me out to the ball game,
Take me out with the crowd,
Buy me some peanuts and cracker jack,
I don't care if I never get back,
Let me root, root, root for the home team,
If they don't win it's a shame,
For it's one, two, three strikes, you're out,
At the old ball game."

Katie Casey saw all the games,
Knew the players by their first names,

Told the umpire he was wrong,
All along good and strong,
When the score was just two to two,
Katie Casey knew what to do,
Just to cheer up the boys she knew,
She made the gang sing this song:

❀

Chorus

On The Road To Mandalay

By the old Moulmein Pagoda,
Looking eastward to the sea,
There's a Burma gal a settin',
And I know that she waits for me.

And the wind is in those palm trees,
And the temple bells they say,
Come you back you mother soldier,
Come you back to Mandalay, come you back,
To Mandalay.

Come you back to Mandalay,
Where the old flotilla lay,
I can here those paddles chonking',
From Rangoon to Mandalay.

On the road to Mandalay,
Where the flying fishes play,
And the dawn comes up like thunder,
Out of China across the bay.

Ship me somewhere east of Suez,
Where the best is like the worst,

And there ain't no Ten Commandments,
   And a cat can raise a thirst.

And those crazy bells keep ringing,
   'Cause it's there that I long to be,
By the Egg Foo Yong Pagoda,
   Looking eastward to the sea.

SHINE ON,
HARVEST MOON

By Jack Norworth

The night was mighty dark so you could hardly see,
For the moon refused to shine,
Couple sitting underneath a willow tree,
For love they did pine,
Little maid was kinda 'fraid of darkness,
So she said, "I guess I'll go,"
Boy began to sigh, looked up at the sky,
And told the moon his little tale of woe.

Chorus:
Oh, shine on, shine on, harvest moon,
Up in the sky,
I ain't had no lovin',
Since January, April, June or July,
Snow time t'ain't no time to stay,
Outdoors and spoon,
Shine on, shine on, harvest moon,
For me and my gal.

I can't see why a boy should sigh,
When by his side is the girl he loves so true,
All he has to say is,
"Won't you be my bride,
For I love you,
I can't see why I'm telling you this secret,
When I know that you can guess."
Harvest moon will smile,
Shine on all the while,
If the little girl should answer "yes."

❧

Chorus

It's A Long Way To Tipperary

By Jack Judge and Henry James Williams

Up to mighty London came an Irishman one day,
As the streets are paved with gold, sure everyone was gay,
Singing songs of Piccadilly, Strand and Leicester Square,
Till Paddy got excited, then he shouted to them there,

Chorus:
"It's a long way to Tipperary,
It's a long way to go,
It's a long way to Tipperary,
To the sweetest girl I know!
Good-bye, Piccadilly! Farewell, Leicester Square!
It's a long, long way to Tipperary,
But my heart's right there!"

Paddy wrote a letter to his Irish Molly O,
Saying, "Should you not receive it,
Write and let me know!
If I make mistakes in spelling, Molly dear," said he,
"Remember it's the pen that's bad,
Don't lay the blame on me."

❧

Chorus

❧

Molly wrote a neat reply to Irish Paddy-O,
Saying, "Mike Mahoney wants to marry me, and so,
Leave the Strand and Piccadilly, or you'll be to blame,
For love has fairly drove me silly, hoping you're the same!"

❧

Chorus

Moonlight Bay

By Edward Madden and Percy Weinrich

We were sailing along on Moonlight Bay,
We could hear the voices ringing,
They seemed to say,
"You have stolen her heart,"
"Now don't go 'way,"
As we sang love's old sweet song on Moonlight Bay.

&

We were sailing along on Moonlight Bay,
We could hear the voices ringing,
They seemed to say,
"You have stolen her heart,"
"Now don't go 'way,"
As we sang love's old sweet song on Moonlight Bay.

&

We were sailing along on Moonlight Bay,
We could hear the voices ringing,
They seemed to say,
"You have stolen her heart" (You have stolen her heart),
"Now don't go 'way,"
As we sang love's old sweet song on Moonlight Bay,
Sailing through the moonlight on Moonlight Bay.

You Made Me Love You
(I Didn't Want to Do It)

By James V. Monaco and Joseph McCarthy

You made me love you,
I didn't want to do it, I didn't want to do it,
You made me love you,
And all the time you knew it,
I guess you always knew it,
You made me happy sometimes, you made me glad,
But there were times, Dear, you made me feel so bad.

❀

You made me sigh for, I didn't want to tell you,
I didn't want to tell you,
I want some love that's true, yes I do, deed I do,
You know I do.

❀

Give me, give me, give me what I cry for,
You know you got the brand of kisses that I'd die for,
You know you made me love you.

For Me And My Gal

By George W. Meyer, Edgar Leslie, and E. Ray Goetz

The bells are ringin', for me and my gal,
The birds are singin' for me and my gal,
Everybody's been knowing, to a wedding they're going,
An' for weeks they've been sewing every Susie and Sal.

❧

They're congregatin' (ding, dong, ding, dong),
For me an' my gal (ding, dong, ding, dong),
The Parson's waitin' (ding, dong, ding, dong),
For me and my gal (ding, dong, ding, dong),
An' someday I'm gonna build a little home for two,
Or three or four, or more,
In Loveland, for me an' my gal.

❧

See the relatives there, lookin' over the pair,
They can tell at a glance, it's a loving romance,
It's a wonderful sight, as the families unite,
See it makes the boy proud, as he says to the crowd:

❧

The bells are ringin', for me and my gal,
The birds are singin' for me and my gal,
Everyone's been knowin' (all our friends and our relations!),

To a weddin' they're goin' (will be at the railroad station!),
An' for weeks they've been sewin',
(Or, they'll send congratulations!),
Every Susie and Sal (for me and my gal!).

✿

They're congregatin' for me and my gal,
The Parson's waitin' for me and my gal,
An' someday I'm gonna build a little home for two,
(Or three or four) or more (or more!),
In Loveland! (Loveland!),
In Loveland! (Loveland!),
In Loveland, for me and my gal!

She Wore a Yellow Ribbon

Round her neck she wore a yellow ribbon,
She wore it in the winter,
And the merry month of May,
When I asked her, why the yellow ribbon?
She said, it's for my lover who is far, far away.

❁

Far away, far away, far away, far away,
She said, It's for my lover who is far, far away,
Far away, far away, far away, far away,
She said, It's for my lover who is far, far away.

❁

When, at first, she met a winsome Johnny,
He wasn't sure her heart was pure,
Her eyes were far too bold,
So, round her neck,
He tied a yellow ribbon,
He tied a yellow ribbon,
'Cause it matched her hair of gold.

❁

Hair of gold, hair of gold,
He tied a yellow ribbon,
'Cause it matched her hair of gold,
Hair of gold, hair of gold,

He tied a yellow ribbon,
For her eyes were far too bold.

❦

If, perchance, you spy a lovely maiden,
And by her side, there walks with pride,
A Johnny strong and gay,
And round her neck there is a yellow ribbon,
No matter how you love her,
Please stay far, far away.

❦

Far away, far away, far away, far away,
No matter how you love her,
Please stay far, far away,
Far away, far away, far away, far away,
Her love is for another,
So stay far, far away,
Far, far away.

Hail, Hail, The Gang's All Here

By D.A. Esrom, Theodore Morse, and Arthur Sullivan

A gang of good fellows are we, (are we),
Are we, (are we) are we, (are we),
With never a worry you see, (you see),
You see, (you see) you see, (you see),
We laugh and joke, we sing and smoke,
And live life merrily,
No matter the weather,
When we get together,
We have a jubilee.

✿

Chorus:
We love one another we do, (we do),
We do, (we do) we do, (we do),
With brotherly love and it's true, (it's true),
It's true, (it's true) it's true, (it's true),
It's one for all, the big and small,
It's always me for you,
No matter the weather,
When we get together,
We drink a toast for two.

✿

Chorus

❦

When out for a good time we go, (we go),
We go, (we go,) we go, (we go),
There nothing we do that is slow, (is slow),
Is slow, (is slow) is slow, (is slow),
Of joy we get our share you bet,
The gang will tell you so,
No matter the weather,
When we get together,
We sing this song you know.

❦

Chorus

❦

Hail! Hail! The gang's all here,
What the deuce do we care,
What the deuce do we care,
Hail! Hail! We're full of cheer,
What the deuce do we care Bill!

❦

Chorus

I Ain't Got Nobody

By Roger Graha, Dave Peyton, and Spencer Williams

There's a sayin' goin' round,
And I begin to think it's true,
It's awful hard to love someone,
When they don't care about you.

Once I had a lovin' man,
As good as any in this town,
But now I'm sad and lonely,
For he's gone and turned me down.

Chorus:
I ain't got nobody, and nobody cares for me!
That's why I'm sad and lonely,
Won't somebody come and take a chance with me?
I'll sing you sweet love songs all the time,
If you'll come and be my sweet baby mine,
I guess I ain't got nobody, nobody cares for me!

If I only had someone,
That I could only call my own,
For I would marry them at once,

And take them to my home,
Every night I sigh and cry,
No happiness at all I find,
I have no one to love me,
No one to content my mind.

❀

Chorus

The Bells of Saint Mary's

By A. Emmett Adams and Douglas Furber

The bells of St. Mary's,
Ah! Hear they are calling,
The young loves, the true loves,
Who come from the sea.

❧

And so, my beloved,
When red leaves are falling,
The love bells shall ring out,
Ring out for you and me.

❧

The bells of St. Mary's,
At sweet even time,
Shall call me, beloved,
To come to your side.

❧

And out in the valley,
In sound of the sea,
I know you'll be waiting,
Yes, waiting for me.

❧

At the porch of St. Mary's,
I'll wait there for you,
In your soft wedding dress,
With its ribbons of blue.

❀

In the church of St. Mary's,
Sweet voices shall sing,
For you and me, dearest,
The wedding bells ring.

Keep the Home Fires Burning

By Ivor Novello and Lena Ford

They were summoned from the hillside,
They were called in from the glen,
And the country found them ready at,
The stirring call for men,
Let no tears add to their hardships,
As the soldiers pass along,
And although your heart is breaking,
Make it sing this cheery song.

❀

Chorus:
Keep the home fires burning,
While your hearts are yearning,
Though your lads are far away they dream of home,
There's a silver lining, through the dark clouds shining,
Turn the dark cloud inside out, 'til the boys come home.

❀

Overseas there came a pleading,
"Help a nation in distress."
And we gave our glorious laddies,
Honor bade us do no less,

For no gallant son of freedom to a tyrant's,
Yoke should bend,
And a noble heart must answer to,
The sacred call of "Friend."

❧

Chorus

MacNamara's Band

My name is MacNamara,
I'm the leader of a band,
And though we're small in number,
We're the best in all the land,
Of course I'm the conductor,
And I've often had to play,
With all the fine musicians,
That you read about today.

❀

Oh! The drums go bang,
And the crystals clang,
And the horns they blaze away,
Macarthy puffs the ould bassoon,
Doyle (and I) the pipes does play,
Hennessey tuteily tootles the flute,
The music is something grand,
And a credit to ould Ireland's boys,
Is MacNamara's Band.

❀

Whenever an election's on,
We play on either side,
And the way we play the fine ould airs,
Fills every heart with pride,

If dear Tom Moore was living now,
He'd make them understand,
That none can do him justice,
Like ould MacNamara's Band.

❀

We play for fairs or weddings,
And for every county ball,
And at any great man's funeral,
We play "The Dead March in Saul,"
When General Grant to Ireland came,
He shook me by the hand,
And said he never heard the like,
Of ould MacNamara's Band.

❀

Just now we are practicing,
For a very grand affair,
It's an annual celebration,
All the gentry will be there,
The girls and boys will all turn out,
With flags and colours grand,
And in front of the procession,
Will be MacNamara's Band.

OVER THERE

By George M. Cohan

Johnnie get your gun, get your gun, get your gun,
Take it on the run, on the run, on the run,
Hear them calling you and me,
Every son of Liberty,
Hurry right away, no delay, go today,
Make your daddy glad to have had such a lad,
Tell your sweetheart not to pine,
To be proud her boy's in line.

Johnnie get your gun, get your gun, get your gun,
Johnnie show the Hun, you're a son-of-a-gun,
Hoist the flag and let her fly,
Like true heroes do or die,
Pack your little kit, show your grit, do your bit,
Soldiers to the ranks from the towns and the tanks,
Make your Mother proud of you and to Liberty be true.

Over There,
Over There,
Send the word, send the word,
Over There,

That the Yanks are coming,
The Yanks are coming,
The drums rum tumming everywhere,
So prepare,
Say a Prayer,
Send the word,
Send the word to beware,
We'll be over, we're coming over,
And we won't be back till it's over over there!
Over There,
Over There,
Send the word, send the word,
Over There,
That the Yanks are coming,
The Yanks are coming,
The drums rum tumming everywhere,
So prepare,
Say a prayer,
Send the word,
Send the word to beware,
We'll be over, we're coming over,
And we won't be back till,
It's over over there!

Pack Up Your Troubles in Your Old Kit Bag

By George Asaf and Felix Powell

Pack up your troubles in your old kit bag,
And smile, smile, smile,
Don't let your joy and laughter hear the snag,
Smile boys, that's the style.

❀

Chorus:
What's the use of worrying,
It never was worth while,
So, pack up your troubles in your old kit bag,
And smile, smile, smile.

❀

Pack up your troubles in your old kit bag,
And smile, smile, smile,
Just pucker up and whistle.

❀

Chorus

Pretty Baby

By Tony Jackson, Gus Kahn, and Egbert Van Alstyne

You ask me why I'm always teasing you,
You hate to have me call you "Pretty Baby,"
I really thought that I was pleasing you,
For you're just a baby to me,
Your cunning little dimples and your baby stare,
Your baby talk and baby walk and curly hair,
Your baby smile makes life worth while,
You're just as sweet as you can be.

Your mother says you were the cutest kid,
No wonder, dearie, that I'm wild about you,
And all the cunning things you said and did,
Why, I love to fondly recall,
And just like Peter Pan, it seems you'll always be,
The same sweet, cunning, Little Baby dear to me,
And that is why I'm sure that I will always,
Love you best of all.

Everybody loves a baby that's why I'm in love with you,
Pretty Baby, Pretty Baby,
And I'd to be your sister, brother, dad, and mother, too,

Pretty Baby, Pretty Baby,
Won't you come and let me rock you in,
My cradle of love,
And we'll cuddle all the time,
Oh! I want a lovin' baby and it might as well be you,
Pretty Baby of mine.

Roses of Picardy

By Frederic E. Weatherly and Hayden Wood

She is watching by the poplars,
Colinette with the sea-blue eyes,
She is watching and longing, and waiting,
Where the long white roadway lies,
And a song stirs in the silence,
As the wind in the boughs above,
She listens and starts and trembles,
'Tis the first little song of love.

Chorus:
Roses are shining in Picardy,
In the hush of the silver dew,
Roses are flow'ring in Picardy,
But there's never a rose like you!
And the roses will die with the summertime,
And our roads may be far apart,
But there's one rose that dies not in Picardy,
'Tis the rose that I keep in my heart.

And the years fly on forever,
Till the shadows veil their skies,

But he loves to hold her little hands,
And look into her sea-blue eyes,
And she sees the road by the poplars,
Where they met in the bygone years,
For the first little song of the roses,
Is the last little song she hears.

❀

Chorus

Till the Clouds Roll By

By Jerome Kern and P.G. Wodehouse

She:
I'm so sad to think that I had to,
Drive you from home so coolly.

※

He:
I'd be gaining nothing by remaining,
What would Mrs. Grundy say?
Her conventions, kindly recollect them!
We must please respect them duly.

※

She:
My intrusion needs explaining,
I felt my courage waning,
Please, I beg don't mention it!
But it has started raining.

※

Both:
Oh, the rain comes a pitter, patter,
And I'd like to be safe in bed,
Skies are weeping, while the world is sleeping,
Trouble heaping on our head,

It is vain to remain and chatter,
And to wait for a clearer sky,
Helter-skelter, I must fly for shelter,
Till the clouds roll by.

❀

She:
What bad luck, It's coming down in buckets,
Have you an umbrella handy?

❀

He:
I've a warm coat, waterproof, a storm coat,
I shall be alright, I know,
Later on, too, I will ward the grippe off,
With a little nip of brandy.

❀

She:
Or a glass of toddy draining,
You'd find that more sustaining,
Don't be worried, I entreat,
I've rubbers for my feet,
So I don't mind it raining.

❀

Both:
Oh, the rain comes a pitter, patter,
And I'd like to be safe in bed,
Skies are weeping, while the world is sleeping,

Trouble heaping on our head,
It is vain to remain and chatter,
And to wait for a clearer sky,
Helter-skelter, I must fly for shelter,
Till the clouds roll by.

Will You Remember

By Sigmund Romberg
and Rida Johnson Young

Ah, love is so sweet in the Springtime,
When blossoms are fragrant in May,
No years that are coming can bring time,
To make me forget dear, this day.

❧

I love you in life's gray December,
The same as I love you today,
My heart ever young will remember,
The thrill it knew, that day in May.

❧

Sweetheart, sweetheart, sweetheart,
Will you love me ever?
Will you remember this day?
When we were happy in May,
My dearest one.

❧

Sweetheart, sweetheart, sweetheart,
Though our paths may sever,
To life's last faint ember,
Will you remember?

Springtime, lovetime, May,
Springtime, lovetime, May.

Under the Yum Yum Tree

By Andrew B. Sterling and Harry Von Tilzer

There's a place to go, where the breezes blow,
And the hum of the bumble-bee,
As he buzzes by,
'Neath a tinted sky,
In a sweet honeyed melody,
Take your sweet heart true, to this place with you,
There's a spot where no one can see,
You can lovey, lovey, love,
With your dovey, dovey, dove,
Under the Yum Yum tree.

Chorus:
Under the Yum Yum tree,
That's the yummiest place to be,
When you take you baby, by the hand,
There'll be something doing down in,
Yum Yum land,
That is the place to play,
With you honey, and kiss all day,
When you're all by your lonely,

You and your only,
Yum! Yum! yummy, yummy,
Yum under the Yum Yum tree.

❀

Thee Yum Yum tree just grew, in the land of "Coo,"
It was planted by old King "Spoon,"
Even birds that fly, in it's branches high,
Sing a soft little loving tune,
Cupid and his band haunt that goo-goo land,
And a dart in your heart there'll be,
If you spoony, spoony, spoon,
'Neath the moony, moony, moon,
Under the Yum Yum tree.

❀

Chorus

Wait Till the Sun Shines, Nellie

By Andrew B. Sterling and Harry Von Tilzer

On a Sunday, sat a maiden forlorn,
With her sweetheart by her side,
Through the window pane she looked at the rain,
"We must stay home, Joe," she cried,
"There's a picnic too, at the old point view,
It's a shame it rained today."

❀

Then the boy drew near, kissed away each tear,
And she heard him softly say.

❀

Chorus:
"Wait till the sun shines, Nellie,
When the clouds go drifting by,
We will be happy, Nellie,
Don't you sigh,
Down lover's lane we'll wander,
Sweethearts you and I,
So won't you wait till the sun shines, Nellie,
By and by."

❀

"How I long," she sighed "for a trolley ride,
Just to show my brand new gown."
Then she gazed on high with a gladsome cry,
For the sun came shining down.
And she looked so sweet on the big front seat.

❧

As the car sped on its way,
And she whispered low, "Say, you're all right, Joe,
You just won my heart today."

❧

Chorus

By the Waters of Minnetonka

By J.M. Cavanass and Thurlow Lieurance

Moon Deer,
How near,
Your soul divine!
Sun Deer,
No fear,
In heart of mine.

Skies blue,
Over you,
Look down in love,
Waves bright,
Give light,
As on they move.

Hear thou,
My vow,
To live to die,
Moon Deer,
Thee near,
Beneath this sky.

Missouri Waltz

By Frederick Knight Logan and James Royce Shannon

Hush-a-bye m'baby, slumber time is comin' soon,
Rest your head upon my breast while Mammy,
Hums a tune,
The sandman is callin' where shadows are fallin',
While the soft breezes sigh as in days long gone by!

❀

Chorus:
Way down in Missouri, where I heard this melody,
When I was a little boy upon my Mammy's knee,
The old-folks were hummin' and the banjos,
Were strummin',
So sweet and low!

❀

Strum, strum, strum, strum, strum!
Seems I hear those banjos playin' once again,
Hmmm, hum, hmmm!
That same old plaintive phrase!

❀

Chorus

Play a Simple Melody

By Irving Berlin

Won't you play some simple melody,
Like my mother sang to me,
One with a good old-fashioned harmony,
Play some simple melody.

Musical demon, set your honey a–dreaming,
Won't you play me some rag,
Just change that classical nag to some sweet beautiful drag,
If you will play from a copy of a tune that is choppy,
You'll get all my applause,
And that is simply because I want to listen to rag.

Play for me,
That good old-fashioned harmony,
Oh, won't you play for me,
A simple melody.

Play from a copy of a tune that is choppy,
You'll get all of my applause because,
I want to rag it,
Ragtime melody.

Sylvia

By Oley Speaks

Sylvia's hair is like the night,
Touched with glancing starry beams,
Such a face as drifts thro' dreams,
This is Sylvia to the sight,
And the touch of Sylvia's hand is as light,
As milkweed down,
When the meads are golden brown,
And the autumn fills the land,
Silvia just the echoing,
Of her voice brings back to me,
From the depths of memory,
All the loveliness of spring,
Sylvia! Sylvia!
Such a face as drifts through dreams,
This is Sylvia to the sight.

When You Wore a Tulip

By Percy Wenrich and Jack Mahoney

When you wore a tulip,
A sweet yellow tulip,
And I wore a big red rose,
When you caressed me,
'Twas then Heaven blessed me,
What a blessing, no one knows,
You made life cheery,
When you called me dearie,
'Twas down where the blue grass grows,
Your lips were sweeter than julep,
When you wore that tulip,
And I wore a big red rose.

I'm Just Wild About Harry

By Noble Sissle and Eubie Blake

There's just one fellow for me in this world,
Harry's his name,
That's what I claim,
Why for ev'ry fellow there must be a girl,
I've found my mate, by kindness of fate.

I'm just wild about Harry,
And Harry's wild about me,
The heav'nly blisses of his kisses,
Fill me with ecstasy,
He's sweet, just like choc'late candy,
And just like honey from the bee,
Oh, I'm just wild about Harry,
And he's just wild about,
Cannot do without,
He's just wild about me.

Ain't We Got Fun?

By Gus Kahn, Raymond Egan, and Richard Whiting

Bill collectors gather,
'Round and rather,
Haunt the cottage next door,
Men the grocer and butcher sent,
Men who call for the rent,
But within a happy chappy,
And his bride of only a year,
Seem to be so cheerful,
Here's an earful,
Of the chatter you hear.

❀

Chorus:
Every morning,
Every evening,
Ain't we got fun?
Not much money,
Oh! But honey,
Ain't we got fun?
The rent's unpaid, dear,
We haven't a car,
But anyway, dear,

We'll stay as we are,
Even if owe the grocer,
Don't we have fun,
Tax collector's getting closer,
Still we have fun,
There's nothing surer,
The rich get richer and the poor get poorer,
In the meantime, in between time,
Ain't we got fun?

❀

Just to make their trouble,
Nearly double,
Something happen'd last night,
To their chimney a gray bird came,
Mister Stork is his name,
And I'll bet two pins,
A pair of twins,
Just happened in with the bird,
Still they're very gay and merry,
Just at dawning I heard:

❀

Chorus

HOME SWEET HOME

By John H. Payne and Henry R. Bishop

'Mid pleasures and palaces,
Though we may roam,
Be it ever so humble,
There's no place like home,
A charm from the skies,
Seems to hallow us there,
Which seek through the world,
Is never met with elsewhere.

❁

Chorus:
Home, home, sweet sweet home,
There's no place like home,
There's no place like home.

❁

I gaze on the moon,
As I tread the drear wild,
And feel that my mother,
Now thinks of her child,
As she looks on that moon,
From our own cottage door,

Thro' the woodbine whose fragrance,
Shall cheer me no more.

※

Chorus

※

An exile from home,
Splendor dazzles in vain,
Oh, give me my lowly,
Thatched cottage again,
The birds singing gaily,
That came at my call,
Give me them and that,
Peace of mind, dearer than all.

※

Chorus

The Marine's Hymn

From the halls of Montezuma,
To the shores of Tripoli,
We will fight our country's battles,
In the air, on land and sea,
First to fight for right and freedom,
And to keep our honor clean,
We are proud to claim the title,
Of United States Marines.

❦

Our flag's unfurl'd to e'ery breeze,
From dawn to setting sun,
We have fought in ev'ry clime and place,
Where we could take a gun,
In the snow of far off northern lands,
And in sunny tropic scenes,
You will find us always on the job,
The United States Marines.

❦

Here's health to you and to our corps,
Which we are proud to serve,
In many a strife we've fought for life,
And never lost our nerve,
If the Army and the Navy,

Ever look on Heaven's scenes,
They will find the streets are guarded,
By United States Marines.

FUNICULI, FUNICULA

Some think the world is made for fun and frolic,
And so do I! And so do I!
Some think it well to be all melancholic,
To pine and sigh, to pine and sigh,
But I, I love to spend my time in singing,
Some joyous song, some joyous song,
To set the air with music bravely ringing,
Is far from wrong, is far from wrong.

Chorus:
Harken! Harken! Music sounds afar!
Harken! Harken! Music sounds afar!
Tralalala Tralalala,
Tralalala Tralalala,
Joy is everywhere,
Funiculi, Funicula!

Ah me! 'Tis strange that some should take to sighing,
And like it well, and like it well,
For me, I have not thought it worth the trying,
So cannot tell, so cannot tell,
With laugh and dance and song the day soon passes,
Full soon is gone, full soon is gone,

For mirth was made for joyous lads and lasses,
  To call their own, to call their own.

❀

Chorus

My Country 'Tis of Thee

My country, 'tis of thee,
Sweet land of liberty,
Of thee I sing,
Land where my fathers died,
Land of the pilgrims' pride,
From every mountainside,
Let freedom ring!

My native country, thee,
Land of the noble free,
Thy name I love,
I love thy rocks and rills,
Thy woods and templed hills,
My heart with rapture thrills,
Like that above.

Let music swell the breeze,
And ring from all the trees,
Sweet freedom's song,
Let mortal tongues awake,
Let all that breath partake,
Let rocks their silence break,
The sound prolong.

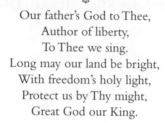

Our father's God to Thee,
Author of liberty,
To Thee we sing.
Long may our land be bright,
With freedom's holy light,
Protect us by Thy might,
Great God our King.

I've Been Working On The Railroad

I've been working on the railroad,
All the livelong day,
I've been working on the railroad,
Just to pass the time away.

Can't you hear the whistle blowing,
Rise up so early in the morn,
Can't you hear the captain shouting,
Dinah, blow your horn.

Dinah, won't you blow,
Dinah, won't you blow,
Dinah, won't you blow your horn,
Dinah, won't you blow,
Dinah, won't you blow,
Dinah, won't you blow your horn.

Someone's in the kitchen with Dinah,
Someone's in the kitchen I know,
Someone's in the kitchen with Dinah,
Strumming on the old banjo, and singing:

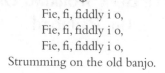

Fie, fi, fiddly i o,
Fie, fi, fiddly i o,
Fie, fi, fiddly i o,
Strumming on the old banjo.

Wabash Cannonball

By J. A. Roff

From the wide Pacific Ocean to the broad Atlantic shore,
She climbs the flowery mountains,
Or'er hills and by the shore,
Though she's tall and handsome and,
She's known quite well by all,
She's a regular combination, on the Wabash Cannonball.

❀

Oh the Eastern states are dandy,
So the Western people say,
From New York to St. Louis by the way,
To the lakes of Minnesota where the rippling waters fall,
No chances to be taken on the Wabash Cannonball.

❀

Listen to the jingle, the rumble and the roar,
As she glides along the woodland,
Over hills and by the shore,
Hear the mighty rush of the engine, hear the crazy
hobos yell while travelling through the jungle,
On the Wabash Cannonball.

❀

Oh, here's old daddy Cleaton, let his name forever be,
And long be remembered in the courts of Tennessee,

For he is a good old rounder 'til the,
Curtain round him fall,
He'll be carried back to victory on the
Wabash Cannonball.

❀

I have rode the I.C. Limited, also the Royal Blue,
Across the Eastern counties on Elkhorn Number Two,
I have rode these highball trains from,
Coast to coast that's all,
But I have found no equal to the Wabash Cannonball.

❀

Oh, listen to the jingle, the rumble and the roar,
As she glides along the woodland,
Over hills and by the shore,
She climbs the flowery mountains,
Hear the merry hobo squall,
As she glides along the woodland,
On the Wabash Cannonball.

Streets of Loredo

By Francis Maynard

"As I walked out in the streets of Loredo,
As I walked in to old Loredo Town,
I spied a poor cowboy all wrapped in white linen,
All wrapped in white linen for they had
gunned him down."

❀

"Oh, I see by your outfit you are a cowpuncher,"
This poor boy said from his lips of flame red,
"They done gunned me down, boys,
And run off and left me,
Here in the back street just like I was dead."

❀

"Well, I see by your outfit you are a cowpuncher,"
This poor boy says as I boldly step by,
"Come sit down beside me, my story I'll tell you,
Cause I'm a poor cowboy and I'm going to die."

❀

"Well, I was born in Southeast Texas,
Where the jimson weed and the lilac does bloom,
I went to go live there for to go far a-ranging,
And I've trailed from Canady down to old Mexico."

" 'Twas once in the saddle I used to go dashing,
'Twas once in the saddle I used to go gay,
'Twas first down to the dram house and,
Then down to Maisy's,
I'se shot in the breast and I'm dying today."

❧

"Well, go write a letter to my grey-haired mother,
Go pen me a note to my sister so dear,
But there is another more dear than a mother,
Who'll bitterly weep when she knows that I'm hurt."

❧

"Get sixteen cowboys to carry my coffin,
Get sixteen pretty ladies to bear up my pall,
Put roses all over the top of my coffin,
To deaden the smell as they bear me along."

❧

"Oh, swing the rope slowly and ring your spurs lowly,
And play the dead march as you bear me along,
Take me to the green valley, there lay the sod o'er me,
'Cause I'm a poor cowboy and I know
I've done wrong."

CLEMENTINE

By Percey Montross

In a cavern, in a canyon,
Excavating for a mine,
Dwelt a miner forty niner,
And his daughter Clementine.

Chorus:
Oh my darling, oh my darling,
Oh my darling, Clementine!
Thou art lost and gone forever,
Dreadful sorry, Clementine.

Light she was and like a fairy,
And her shoes were number nine,
Herring boxes, without topses,
Sandals were for Clementine.

Chorus

Drove she ducklings to the water,
Ev'ry morning just at nine,

Hit her foot against a splinter,
Fell into the foaming brine.

🌸

Chorus

🌸

Ruby lips above the water,
Blowing bubbles, soft and fine,
But, alas, I was no swimmer,
So I lost my Clementine.

🌸

Chorus

🌸

How I missed her! How I missed her,
How I missed my Clementine,
But I kissed her little sister,
I forgot my Clementine.

🌸

Chorus

CHAPTER

8

THE BLUES

PEOPLE have been getting the blues about one thing or another since the world began, but it only became a musical style around the turn of the twentieth century. Although African-Americans in many parts of the South had been composing and playing their own blues for many years, it wasn't until W.C. Handy (1873–1958) started publishing compositions based partly on their styles and lyrics, that the music became nationally known.

Handy gave us "St. Louis Blues" (page 466), "Beale Street Blues" (page 462), "Aunt Hagar's Blues" (page 476) and many others still known and loved today. In his footsteps followed Perry Bradford, Spencer Williams, and a host of other early blues composers.

The Blues became one of the first styles to "cross over" to mainstream audiences, as white singers like Sophie Tucker and Marion Harris put the blues on record in the 1910s, and black singers like Bessie Smith made records that sold with all audiences in the 1920s.

The early blues in this section are often ironic or humorous, and were favorites of the vaudeville stage, but sorrow was never far—as many a blues singer of the period liked to tell their audience, "I'm laughin' to keep from cryin'!"

BEALE STREET BLUES

By W.C. Handy

I've seen the lights of gay Broadway,
Old Market Street down by the Frisco Bay,
I've strolled the Prado, I've gambled on the Bourse,
The seven wonders of the world I've seen,
And many are the places I have been,
Take my advice, folks, and see Beale Street first!

You'll see pretty browns in beautiful gowns,
You'll see tailor-mades and hand-me-downs,
You'll meet honest men, and pick-pockets skilled,
You'll find that business never ceases 'til,
Somebody gets killed!

If Beale Street could talk, if Beale Street could talk,
Married men would have to take their beds and walk,
Except one or two who never drink booze,
And the blind man on the corner singing,
"Beale Street Blues!"

I'd rather be there than any place I know,
I'd rather be there than any place I know,
It's gonna take a sergeant for to make me go!

I'm goin' to the river, maybe by and by,
Yes, I'm goin' to the river, maybe by and by,
Because the river's wet, and,
Beale Street's done gone dry!

CRAZY BLUES

By Perry Bradford

I can't sleep at night,
I can't eat a bite,
'Cause the man I love,
He don't treat me right.

He makes me feel so blue,
I don't what to do,
Sometimes I sit and cry,
And then begin to sigh,
'Cause my best friend,
Said his last goodbye.

There's a change in the ocean,
Change in the deep blue sea,
I tell you folks there ain't no change in me,
My love for that man will always be.

Now I got the crazy blues,
Since my baby went away,
I ain't got no time to lose,
I must find him today.

❀

Now the doctor's gonna do all that he can,
But what he's gonna need is the undertaker man,
I ain't had nothing but bad news,
Now I got the crazy blues.

❀

I can read his letters,
I sure can't read his mind,
I thought he was lovin' me,
He's leavin' all the time,
Now I see my poor love was blind.

❀

I went to the railroad,
Set my head down on the track,
Thought about my daddy,
And I snatched it back,
Now he's gone and gave me the sack.

❀

Now I got the crazy blues,
Since my baby went away,
I ain't got no time to lose,
I must find him today.

ST. LOUIS BLUES

By W.C. Handy

I hate to see that evening sun go down,
I hate to see that evening sun go down,
'Cause my lovin' baby done left this town.

❀

If I feel tomorrow, like I feel today,
If I feel tomorrow, like I feel today,
I'm gonna pack my trunk and make my getaway.

❀

Oh, that St. Louis woman, with her diamond rings,
She pulls my man around by her apron strings,
And if it wasn't for powder and her store-bought hair,
Oh, that man wouldn't go nowhere.

❀

I got those St. Louis blues, just as blue as I can be,
Oh, my man's got a heart like a rock cast in the sea,
Or else he wouldn't have gone so far from me.

❀

I love my man like a schoolboy loves his pie,
Like a Kentucky colonel loves his rocker and rye,
I'll love my man until the day I die, Lord, Lord.

❀

I got the St. Louis blues, just as blue as
I can be, Lord, Lord!
That man's got a heart like a rock cast in the sea,
Or else he wouldn't have gone so far from me.

❀

I got those St. Louis blues, I got the blues,
I got the blues, I got the blues,
My man's got a heart like a rock cast in the sea,
Or else he wouldn't have gone so far
from me, Lord, Lord!

TISHOMINGO BLUES

By Spencer Williams

Oh, Mississippi,
Oh, Mississippi,
My heart cries out for,
You in sadness,
I want to be where,
The wintry winds don't blow,
Down where the southern moon swings low,
That's where I want to go.

Chorus:
I'm goin' to Tishomingo,
Because I'm sad today,
I wish to linger,
'Way down old Dixie way.
Oh, my weary heart cries out in pain,
Oh, how I wish that I was back again,
With a race,
In a place,
Where they make you welcome all the time,
Way down in Mississippi,
Among the cypress trees,

They get you dippy,
With their strange melodies,
To resist temptation,
I just can't refuse,
In Tishomingo,
I wish to linger,
Where they play the weary blues.

❧

Tonight I'm prayin',
Tonight I'm sayin',
Oh Lord please take the,
Train that takes me,
To Tishomingo,
'Way down old Dixie way,
Where southern folks are,
Always gay,
That's why you hear me say:

❧

Chorus

WICKED BLUES

By Perry Bradford

What must I do, I feel so blue,
Since my cruel baby went away,
Something is wrong, my appetite's gone,
He caught a train and can't be found.

※

And I've got a roamin' mind for to leave this town,
I am worried deep down in my heart today,
I have cried, I have sighed, he went away, never said goodbye,
And the day I see him he will surely die.

※

Now I've got the wicked blues,
'Cause my baby went away,
If I thought he loved me true,
I would have asked him to please stay,
I will buy a gun as long as my right arm,
Shoot at everybody done me any wrong,
Now babe I am all confused,
'Cause I've got the wicked blues.

※

Since he has gone I am alone,
Way deep down in my very heart,

I miss him each day since he went away,
I know the best of friends must part,
And I know he never loved me right from the start.

❦

And I know he never loved me right from the start,
I am worried deep down in my heart today,
I have cried, I have sighed, he went away,
Never said goodbye,
And the day I see him he will surely die.

❦

Now I've got the wicked blues,
'Cause my baby went away,
If I thought he loved me true,
I would have asked him to please stay,
I will buy a gun as long as my right arm,
Shoot at everybody done me any wrong,
Now babe I am all confused,
'Cause I've got the wicked blues.

LOVELESS LOVE

By W.C. Handy

Love is like a gold brick in a bunco game,
Like a banknote with a bogus name,
Both have caused many downfalls,
Love has done the same.

Love has for its emblem Cupid with his bow,
Loveless love has lots and lots of dough,
So carry lots of Jack and pick 'em as you go.

For love, oh love, oh loveless love,
Has set our hearts on goalless goals,
From milkless milk, and silkless silk,
We are growing used to soulless souls,
Such grafting times we never saw,
That's why we have a pure food law,
In everything we find a flaw,
Even love, oh love, oh loveless love.

Love is like a hydrant, it turns off and on,
Like some friendships when your money's gone,
Love stands in with loan sharks when your heart's in pawn,

If I had some strong wings like an aeroplane,
Had some broad wings like an aeroplane,
I would fly away forever ne'er to come again.

❧

Love, oh love, oh loveless love,
You set our hearts on goalless goals,
With dreamless dreams and schemeless schemes,
We wreck out love boats on the shoals,
We S.O.S. by wireless wire,
And in the wreckage of desire,
We sigh for wings like Noah's dove,
Just to fly away from loveless love.

THE HESITATING BLUES

By W.C. Handy

Hello Central, what's the matter with this line?
I want to talk to that high brown of mine,
Tell me how long will I have to wait?
Please give me Two-Nine-Eight,
Why do you hesitate?

What you say, can't talk to my brown!
A storm last night blowed the wires all down,
Tell me how long will I have to wait?
Oh won't you tell me now,
Why do you hesitate?

Chorus:
Procrastination is the thief of time,
So all the wise owls say,
One stitch in time may save nine,
Tomorrow's not today,
And if you put off,
Somebody's bound to lose,
I'd be his, he'd by mine,
And I'd be feeling gay,

Left alone to grieve and pine,
My best friend's done away,
He's gone and left me,
The hesitating blues.

❧

Sunday night my beau proposed to me,
Said he'd be happy if his wifie I'd be,
Said he "How long will I have to wait?
Come be my wife Kate,
Why do you hesitate?"
I declined him just for a stall,
He left that night on the Cannon Ball,
Honey how long will I have to wait?
Will he come back now,
Or will he hesitate?

❧

Chorus

AUNT HAGAR'S BLUES

By W.C. Handy

Old Deacon Splivin, his flock was givin',
The way of living right.

Said he:
"No wingin', no ragtime singin' tonight!"
Up jumped Aunt Hagar and shouted out with all her might,
"Oh 'tain't no use o' preachin',
Oh 'tain't no use o' teachin',
Each modulation of syncopation,
Just tells my feet to dance and I can't refuse,
When I hear the melody they call the blues,
Those ever lovin' blues."

Just hear Aunt Hagar's children harmonizin',
To that old mournful tune,
It's like a choir from on high broke loose,
If the devil brought it,
The good Lord sent it right down to me,
Let the congregation join,
While I sing those lovin' Aunt Hagar's Blues.

LONESOME BLUES

By Perry Bradford

Want someone to love me,
Want someone to hug me now,
Want someone to squeeze me,
Want someone to teach me how,
I don't want your money, all I want my honey is you.

Chorus:
Woke up this morning feeling awfully blue,
Ain't got no one to tell my trouble to,
The fortune-teller,
Has told me little fellow,
That I am lonely, lonely,
And I've got those lonesome blues.

Look here little daddy how I wish you had me dear,
When you're 'way I'm lonely,
That is why I want you near,
Honey please don't leave me,
You will surely grieve me dear.

Chorus

EVERYBODY'S CRAZY 'BOUT THE DOGGONE BLUES, BUT I'M HAPPY

By Henry Creamer and Turner Layton

Blues ain't nothin' but the easygoing heart disease,
Brother stop your moanin',
Blues can't make you warmer if you're bound to freeze,
Sister stop your groanin',
Why don't you rise and shine,
Take them blues right off your 'mind, 'cause,
The blues ain't nothin' but the easygoing heart disease,
That's all!

Chorus:
Everybody's crazy 'bout the doggone blues,
But I'm happy, oh so happy,
Everybody's crazy but if I must choose,
No doggone blues for mine,
I get plenty to eat,
I never worry,
Shoes on my feet, don't have to hurry,
I'm not afraid, my rent is paid,

And I can sleep at ninety-four in the shade,
Everybody's singing a lotta bad old news but I'm happy,
Oh so happy!
Life's too doggone short to weep and whine,
Those homesickness blues, take 'em away!
Everybody's crazy about the doggone blues,
But I'm happy all the time!

❧

You all know how Mister Jonah got into that whale,
He fell into the ocean,
There's one man who should have sung blues but failed,
Never had the notion,
Old Jonah knew those whales,
Instead of blues, he ragged the scales,
Then the whale got gay and let old Jonah,
Slip right out of jail!

❧

Chorus

CHAPTER
9

Christmas Songs

WHEN people gather during the Christmas season and go caroling door to door, they are part of an historic tradition. In ancient times, a "carol" was simply a song sung by a group in public, usually in a circle. This custom of carol singing proved especially appropriate and satisfying at Christmas, and countless songs in many languages have been composed over the centuries.

Puritans and others in England and America found these seasonal practices insufficiently reverent and an invitation to bad behavior, but in spite of their best efforts to stamp them out, Christmas carols have endured. Although the coming of the Industrial Revolution and the growth of cities led to the decline of many rural folk singing traditions, Christmas caroling and other seasonal customs seem to have grown stronger. This was a common musical bond that all could share in.

When Charles Dickens published *A Christmas Carol* in 1843, a Christmas music renaissance was well underway. Many of our best-loved Christmas songs were written in the nineteenth century, and reflect those times. Horse drawn sleighs were outfitted with bells to warn pedestrians, and this sound was a seasonal marker in colder climates. Sleighs are mostly gone, but the bells remain, and we celebrate them every time we sing the 1857 classic "Jingle Bells" (page 504). Gone, too, are the days when December 25th was only the beginning of a festal tide that lasted almost two weeks, during which children were rewarded for memorizing musical lists of unusual items, yet we still sing "The Twelve Days of Christmas" (page 518).

Nowadays, the Christmas season seems to begin in late November, so we have included the Thanksgiving song "Over the River" (page 513) to get you in the holiday spirit.

So be of good cheer, and when you sing these songs think not only of their message, but also of the countless anonymous carolers who have kept them alive through the generations.

Merry Christmas!

O Come, All Ye Faithful

O come, all ye faithful, joyful and triumphant,
Oh come ye, O come ye to Bethlehem,
Come and behold him, born the King of angels,
O come, let us adore Him, Christ the Lord.
O come, let us adore Him, Christ the Lord.
O come, let us adore Him, Christ the Lord.

God of God, light of light,
Lo, he abhors not the virgin's womb,
Very God, begotten not created,
O come, let us adore Him, Christ the Lord.
O come, let us adore Him, Christ the Lord.
O come, let us adore Him, Christ the Lord.

Sing, choirs of angels, sing in exultation,
Sing, all ye citizens of heaven above,
Glory to God in the highest,
O come, let us adore Him, Christ the Lord.
O come, let us adore Him, Christ the Lord.
O come, let us adore Him, Christ the Lord.

See how the shepherds summoned to his cradle,
Leaving their flocks, draw nigh with lowly fear,
We too will thither, bend our joyful footsteps,
    O come, let us adore Him, Christ the Lord.
    O come, let us adore Him, Christ the Lord.
    O come, let us adore Him, Christ the Lord.

✿

Yea, Lord, we greet Thee, born this happy morning,
    Jesus, to Thee be glory given,
Word of the Father, now in flesh appearing,
    O come, let us adore Him, Christ the Lord.
    O come, let us adore Him, Christ the Lord.
    O come, let us adore Him, Christ the Lord.

Adeste Fideles

Adeste Fideles,
Laeti triumphantes,
Venite, venite in Bethlehem,
Natum videte,
Regem angelorum,
Venite adoremus,
Venite adoremus,
Venite adoremus,
Dominum.

❦

Cantet nunc io,
Chorus angelorum,
Cantet nunc aula caelestium,
Gloria, Gloria,
In excelsis Deo,
Venite adoremus,
Venite adoremus,
Venite adoremus,
Dominum.

❦

Ergo qui natus,
Die hodierna,
Jesu, tibi sit Gloria,
Patris aeterni,
Verbum caro factus,
Venite adoremus,
Venite adoremus,
Venite adoremus,
Dominum.

Angels We Have Heard On High

Angels we have heard on high,
Singing sweetly through the night,
And the mountains in reply,
Echoing their brave delight.

❧

Chorus:
Gloria in excelsis Deo.
Gloria in excelsis Deo.

❧

Shepherds, why this jubilee?
Why these songs of happy cheer?
What great brightness did you see?
What glad tiding did you hear?

❧

Chorus

❧

Come to Bethlehem and see,
Him whose birth the angels sing,
Come, adore on bended knee,
Christ, the Lord, the new-born King.

❧

Chorus

❧

See him in a manger laid,
Whom the angels praise above,
Mary, Joseph, lend your aid,
While we raise our hearts in love.

Away in a Manger

Away in a manger,
No crib for His bed,
The little Lord Jesus,
Laid down His sweet head.

❀

The stars in the bright sky,
Looked down where He lay,
The little Lord Jesus,
Asleep on the hay.

❀

The cattle are lowing,
The poor Baby wakes,
But little Lord Jesus,
No crying He makes.

❀

I love Thee, Lord Jesus,
Look down from the sky,
And stay by my side,
'Til morning is nigh.

❀

Be near me, Lord Jesus,
I ask Thee to stay,

Close by me forever,
And love me I pray.

❀

Bless all the dear children,
In Thy tender care,
And take us to heaven,
To live with Thee there.

Deck the Halls

Deck the halls with boughs of holly,
Fa la la la la, la la la la,
Tis the season to be jolly,
Fa la la la la, la la la la,
Don we now our gay apparel,
Fa la la, la la la, la la la,
Troll the ancient Yule tide carol,
Fa la la la la, la la la la.

See the blazing Yule before us,
Fa la la la la, la la la la,
Strike the harp and join the chorus.
Fa la la la la, la la la la,
Follow me in merry measure,
Fa la la la la, la la la la,
While I tell of Yule tide treasure,
Fa la la la la, la la la la.

Fast away the old year passes,
Fa la la la la, la la la la,
Hail the new, ye lads and lasses,
Fa la la la la, la la la la,
Sing we joyous, all together,
Fa la la la la, la la la la.
Heedless of the wind and weather,
Fa la la la la, la la la la.

The First Noel

The First Noel, the Angels did say,
Was to certain poor shepherds in fields as they lay,
In fields where they lay keeping their sheep,
On a cold winter's night that was so deep,
Noel, Noel, Noel, Noel,
Born is the King of Israel!

They looked up and saw a star,
Shining in the East beyond them far,
And to the earth it gave great light,
And so it continued both day and night,
Noel, Noel, Noel, Noel,
Born is the King of Israel!

And by the light of that same star,
Three Wise men came from country far,
To seek for a King was their intent,
And to follow the star wherever it went,
Noel, Noel, Noel, Noel,
Born is the King of Israel!

This star drew nigh to the northwest,
O'er Bethlehem it took its rest,
And there it did both pause and stay,
Right o'er the place where Jesus lay,
Noel, Noel, Noel, Noel,
Born is the King of Israel!

&

Then entered in those wise men three,
Full reverently upon their knee,
And offered there in His presence,
Their gold and myrrh and frankincense,
Noel, Noel, Noel, Noel,
Born is the King of Israel!

&

Then let us all with one accord,
Sing praises to our heavenly Lord,
That hath made Heaven and earth of nought,
And with his blood mankind has bought,
Noel, Noel, Noel, Noel,
Born is the King of Israel!

God Rest Ye Merry Gentlemen

God rest ye merry gentlemen,
Let nothing you dismay,
Remember Christ our Savior,
Was born on Christmas day,
To save us all from Satan's pow'r,
When we were gone astray.

Chorus:
O tidings of comfort and joy,
Comfort and joy,
O tidings of comfort and joy.

From God our heavenly Father,
A blessed angel came,
And unto certain shepherds,
Brought tidings of the same,
How that in Bethlehem was born,
The Son of God by name.

Chorus

The shepherds at those tidings,
Rejoiced much in mind,
And left their flocks a-feeding,
In tempest, storm, and wind,
And went to Bethlehem straightway,
This blessed babe to find.

❀

Chorus

❀

But when to Bethlehem they came,
Whereat this infant lay,
They found him in a manger,
Where oxen feed on hay,
His mother Mary kneeling,
Unto the Lord did pray.

❀

Chorus

❀

Now to the Lord sing praises,
All you within this place,
And with true love and brotherhood,
Each other now embrace,
This holy tide of Christmas,
All others doth deface.

❀

Chorus

Good King Wenceslas

Good King Wenceslas looked out,
On the Feast of Stephen,
When the snow lay round about,
Deep and crisp and even,
Brightly shone the moon that night,
Though the frost was cruel,
When a poor man came in sight,
Gathering winter fuel.

"Hither, page, and stand by me,
If though know'st it, telling,
Yonder peasant, who is he?
Where and what his dwelling?"
"Sire, he lives a good league hence,
Underneath the mountain,
Right against the forest fence,
By Saint Agnes' fountain."

"Bring me flesh, and bring me wine,
Bring me pine logs hither,
Thou and I will see him dine,
When we bear them thither."

Page and monarch, forth they went,
　　Forth they went together,
Thro' the rude wind's wild lament,
　　And the bitter weather.

❧

"Sire, the night is darker now,
　　And the wind blows stronger,
Fails my heart, I know not how,
　　I can go no longer."
"Mark my footsteps, my good page,
　　Tread thou in them boldly,
Though shalt find the winter's rage,
　　Freeze thy blood less coldly."

❧

In his master's steps he trod,
　　Where the snow lay dinted,
Heat was in the very sod,
　　Which the Saint had printed,
Therefore, Christian men, be sure,
　　Wealth or rank possessing,
Ye who now will bless the poor,
　　Shall yourself find blessing.

Hark!
the Herald Angels Sing

Hark! The herald angels sing,
Glory to the newborn King,
Peace on earth, and mercy mild,
God and sinners reconcile,
Joyful, all ye nations, rise,
Join the triumph of the skies,
With the angelic host proclaim,
"Christ is born in Bethlehem,"
Hark! The herald angels sing,
Glory to the newborn King.

Christ, by highest heaven adored,
Christ, the everlasting Lord,
Late in time behold him come,
Offspring of a virgin's womb,
Veiled in flesh the Godhead see,
Hail, the incarnate deity,
Pleased as Man with us to dwell,
Jesus, our Emmanuel!
Hark! The herald angels sing,
Glory to the newborn King.

Hail, the heaven-born prince of peace!
Hail the Son of righteousness!
Light and life to all he brings,
Risen with healing in his wings,
Mild he lays his glory by,
Born that man no more may die,
Born to raise the sons of earth,
Born to give them second birth,
Hark! The herald angels sing,
Glory to the newborn King.

The Holly and the Ivy

The holly and the ivy,
When they are both full grown,
Of all the trees that are in the wood,
The holly bears the crown.

O the rising of the sun,
And the running of the deer,
The playing of the merry organ,
Sweet singing in the choir.

The holly bears a blossom,
As white as lily flower,
And Mary bore sweet Jesus Christ,
To be our sweet Savior.

The holly bears a berry,
As red as any blood,
And Mary bore sweet Jesus Christ,
To do poor sinners good.

The holly bears a prickle,
As sharp as any thorn,

And Mary bore sweet Jesus Christ,
On Christmas day in the morn.

❀

The holly bears a bark,
As bitter as any gall,
And Mary bore sweet Jesus Christ,
For to redeem us all.

❀

The holly and the ivy,
When they are both full grown,
Of all the trees that are in the wood,
The holly bears the crown.

I Saw Three Ships

I saw three ships come sailing in,
On Christmas day, on Christmas day,
I saw three ships come sailing in,
On Christmas day in the morning.

And what was in those ships all three,
On Christmas day, on Christmas day?
And what was in those ships all three,
On Christmas day in the morning?

Our Savior Christ and His lady,
On Christmas day, on Christmas day,
Our Savior Christ and His lady,
On Christmas day in the morning.

Pray whither sailed those ships all three,
On Christmas day, on Christmas day?
Pray whither sailed those ships all three,
On Christmas day in the morning?

O they sailed into Bethlehem,
On Christmas day, on Christmas day,

O they sailed into Bethlehem,
On Christmas day in the morning.

🌼

And all the bells on earth shall ring,
On Christmas day, on Christmas day,
And all the bells on earth shall ring,
On Christmas day in the morning.

🌼

And all the angels in Heaven shall sing,
On Christmas day, on Christmas day,
And all the angels in Heaven shall sing,
On Christmas day in the morning.

🌼

And all the souls on Earth shall sing,
On Christmas day, on Christmas day,
And all the souls on Earth shall sing,
On Christmas day in the morning.

🌼

Then let us all rejoice amain,
On Christmas day, on Christmas day,
Then let us rejoice amain,
On Christmas day in the morning.

It Came Upon
a Midnight Clear

It came upon a midnight clear,
That glorious song of old,
From angels bending near the earth
To touch their harps of gold,
"Peace on the earth, good will to men,
From heaven's all-gracious King!"
The world in solemn stillness lay,
To hear the angels sing.

Still through the cloven skies they come,
With peaceful wings unfurled,
And still their heavenly music floats,
O'er all the weary world,
Above its sad and lowly plains,
They bend on hovering wing,
And ever o'er its Babel sounds,
The blessed angels sing.

But with the woes of sin and strife,
The world has suffered long,
Beneath the angel strain have rolled,

Two thousands years of wrong,
And man, at war with man, hears not,
The love song which they bring,
O hush the noise, ye men of strife,
And hear the angels sing.

❧

For, lo! the days are hastening on,
By prophet bards foretold,
When with the ever-circling years,
Comes round the age of gold,
When peace shall over all the earth,
Its ancient splendours fling,
And the whole world give back the song,
Which now the angels sing.

Jingle Bells

By James Lord Pierpont

Dashing through the snow,
In a one-horse open sleigh,
Through the fields we go,
Laughing all the way,
Bells on bob-tail ring,
Making spirits bright,
What fun it is to ride and sing,
A sleighing song tonight.

Chorus:
Jingle bells, jingle bells,
Jingle all the way,
Oh what fun it is to ride,
In a one-horse open sleigh, O,
Jingle bells, jingle bells,
Jingle all the way,
Oh what fun it is to ride,
In a one-horse open sleigh.

A day or two ago,
I thought I'd take a ride,

And soon Miss Fanny Bright,
Was seated by my side,
The horse was lean and lank,
Misfortune seemed his lot,
We ran into a drifted bank,
And there we got upsot.

❦

Chorus

❦

A day or two ago,
The story I must tell,
I went out on the snow,
And on my back I fell,
A gent was riding by,
In a one-horse open sleigh,
He laughed at me as,
I there sprawling laid,
But quickly drove away.

❦

Chorus

❦

Now the ground is white,
Go it while you're young,
Take the girls along,
And sing this sleighing song,
Just bet a bob-tailed bay,

Two-forty as his speed,
Hitch him to an open sleigh,
And crack! You'll take the lead.

❀

Chorus

Jolly Old Saint Nicholas

Jolly old Saint Nicholas,
Lean your ear this way!
Don't you tell a single soul,
What I'm going to say,
Christmas Eve is coming soon,
Now, you dear old man,
Whisper what you'll bring to me,
Tell me if you can.

❀

When the clock is striking twelve,
When I'm fast asleep,
Down the chimney broad and black,
With your pack you'll creep,
All the stockings you will find,
Hanging in a row,
Mine will be the shortest one,
You'll be sure to know.

❀

Johnny wants a pair of skates,
Susy wants a dolly,
Nellie wants a story book,
She thinks dolls are folly,

As for me, my little brain,
Isn't very bright,
Choose for me, old Santa Claus,
What you think is right.

Joy to the World

By Isaac Watts

Joy to the world, the Lord is come!
Let earth receive her King,
Let every heart prepare Him room,
And heaven and nature sing,
And heaven and nature sing,
And heaven, and heaven, and nature sing.

❀

Joy to the world, the Savior reigns!
Let men their songs employ,
While fields and floods, rocks, hills and plains,
Repeat the sounding joy,
Repeat the sounding joy,
Repeat, repeat, the sounding joy.

❀

No more let sins and sorrows grow,
Nor thorns infest the ground,
He comes to make His blessings flow,
Far as the curse is found,
Far as the curse is found,
Far as, far as, the curse is found.

❀

He rules the world with truth and grace,
And makes the nations prove,
The glories of His righteousness,
And wonders of His love,
And wonders of His love,
And wonders, wonders, of His love.

O Christmas Tree

O Christmas tree, O Christmas tree!
How are thy leaves so verdant!
O Christmas tree, O Christmas tree,
How are thy leaves so verdant!

Not only in the summertime,
But even in winter is thy prime,
O Christmas tree, O Christmas tree,
How are thy leaves so verdant!

O Christmas tree, O Christmas tree,
Much pleasure doth thou bring me!
O Christmas tree, O Christmas tree,
Much pleasure doth thou bring me!

For every year the Christmas tree,
Brings to us all both joy and glee,
O Christmas tree, O Christmas tree,
Much pleasure doth thou bring me!

O Christmas tree, O Christmas tree,
Thy candles shine out brightly!

O Christmas tree, O Christmas tree,
Thy candles shine out brightly!

❀

Each bough doth hold its tiny light,
That makes each toy to sparkle bright,
O Christmas tree, O Christmas tree,
Thy candles shine out brightly!

Over the River

By Lydia Maria Child

Over the river and through the wood,
To grandfather's house we go,
The horse knows the way to carry the sleigh,
Through the white and drifted snow, oh!

Over the river and through the wood,
Oh, how the wind does blow!
It stings the toes and bites the nose,
As over the ground we go.

Over the river and through the wood,
To have a first-rate play,
Oh, hear the bell ring, "ting-a-ling-ling!"
Hurrah for Thanksgiving Day-ay!

Over the river and through the wood,
Trot fast my dapple gray!
Spring over the ground,
Like a hunting hound!
For this is Thanksgiving Day.

Over the river and through the wood,
And straight through the barnyard gate,
We seem to go extremely slow,
It is so hard to wait!

❦

Over the river and through the wood,
Now Grandmother's cap I spy!
Hurrah for fun! Is the pudding done?
Hurrah for the pumpkin pie!

O Little Town of Bethlehem

O little town of Bethlehem, how still we see thee lie,
Above thy deep and dreamless sleep the,
Silent stars go by,
Yet in they dark streets shineth, the everlasting light,
The hopes and fears of all the years are met in,
Thee tonight.

❧

For Christ is born of Mary, and gathered all above,
While mortals sleep the angels keep their,
Watch of wondering love,
O morning stars together, proclaim the holy birth,
And praises sing to God the king,
And peace to men on earth.

❧

How silently, how silently, the wondrous gift is given,
So God imparts to human hearts the
Blessings of his heaven,
No ear may hear his coming, but in this world of sin,
Where meek souls will receive him still,
The dear Christ enters in.

❧

O holy Child of Bethlehem, descend to us we pray,
Cast out our sin and enter in, be born in us today,
We hear the Christmas angels, the great glad tidings tell,
O come to us, abide with us, our Lord Emanuel.

Silent Night

Silent night, holy night,
All is calm, all is bright,
Round yon Virgin, Mother and Child,
Holy Infant so tender and mild,
Sleep in heavenly peace,
Sleep in heavenly peace.

※

Silent night, holy night!
Shepherds quake at the sight,
Glories stream from heaven afar,
Heavenly hosts sing "Alleluia!
Christ, the Saviour is born,
Christ, the Saviour is born."

※

Silent night, holy night,
Son of God, love's pure light,
Radiant beams from Thy holy face,
With the dawn of redeeming grace,
Jesus, Lord, at Thy birth,
Jesus, Lord, at Thy birth.

The Twelve Days of Christmas

On the first day of Christmas,
My true love gave to me,
A partridge in a pear tree.

On the second day of Christmas,
My true love gave to me,
Two turtle doves,
And a partridge in a pear tree.

On the third day of Christmas,
My true love gave to me,
Three French hens,
Two turtle doves,
And a partridge in a pear tree.

On the fourth day of Christmas,
My true love gave to me,
Four calling birds,
Three French hens,
Two turtle doves,
And a partridge in a pear tree.

❦

On the fifth day of Christmas,
My true love gave to me,
Five golden rings!
Four calling birds,
Three French hens,
Two turtle doves,
And a partridge in a pear tree.

❦

On the sixth day of Christmas,
My true love gave to me,
Six geese a-laying,
Five golden rings!
Four calling birds,
Three French hens,
Two turtle doves,
And a partridge in a pear tree.

❦

On the seventh day of Christmas,
My true love gave to me,
Seven swans a-swimming,
Six geese a-laying,
Five golden rings!
Four calling birds,
Three French hens,

Two turtle doves,
And a partridge in a pear tree.

❀

On the eighth day of Christmas,
My true love gave to me,
Eight maids a-milking,
Seven swans a-swimming,
Six geese a-laying,
Five golden rings!
Four calling birds,
Three French hens,
Two turtle doves,
And a partridge in a pear tree.

❀

On the ninth day of Christmas,
My true love gave to me,
Nine ladies waiting,
Eight maids a-milking,
Seven swans a-swimming,
Six geese a-laying,
Five golden rings!
Four calling birds,
Three French hens,
Two turtle doves,
And a partridge in a pear tree.

❀

On the tenth day of Christmas,
My true love gave to me,
Ten lords a-leaping,
Nine ladies waiting,
Eight maids a-milking,
Seven swans a-swimming,
Six geese a-laying,
Five golden rings!
Four calling birds,
Three French hens,
Two turtle doves,
And a partridge in a pear tree.

❧

On the eleventh day of Christmas,
My true love gave to me,
Eleven pipers piping,
Ten lords a-leaping,
Nine ladies waiting,
Eight maids a-milking,
Seven swans a-swimming,
Six geese a-laying,
Five golden rings!
Four calling birds,
Three French hens,
Two turtle doves,
And a partridge in a pear tree.

On the twelfth day of Christmas,
My true love gave to me,
Twelve drummers drumming,
Eleven pipers piping,
Ten lords a-leaping,
Nine ladies waiting,
Eight maids a-milking,
Seven swans a-swimming,
Six geese a-laying,
Five golden rings!
Four calling birds,
Three French hens,
Two turtle doves,
And a partridge in a pear tree.

Up On the Rooftop

Up on the rooftop reindeer pause,
Out jumps good old Santa Claus,
Down through the chimney with lots of toys,
All for the little ones,
Christmas joys.

Chorus:
Ho, ho, ho!
Who wouldn't go!
Ho, ho, ho!
Who wouldn't go!
Up on the rooftop,
Click, click, click,
Down through the chimney with,
Good Saint Nick.

First comes the stocking,
Of little Nell,
Oh, dear Santa,
Fill it well,
Give her a dolly,
That laughs and cries,

One that will open,
And shut her eyes.

❀

Chorus

❀

Next comes the stocking,
Of little Will,
Oh, just see what,
A glorious fill,
Here is a hammer,
And lots of tacks,
Also a ball,
And a whip that cracks.

❀

Chorus

The Wassail Song

Here we come a-wassailing,
Among the leaves so green,
Here we come a-wand'ring,
So fair to be seen.

❁

Chorus:
Love and joy come to you,
And to you your wassail, too,
And God bless you, and send you,
A Happy New Year,
And God send you a Happy New Year.

❁

We are not daily beggars,
That beg from door to door,
But we are neighbors' children,
Whom you have seen before.

❁

Chorus

❁

Good master and good mistress,
As you sit beside the fire,

Pray think of us poor children,
Who wander in the mire.

❀

Chorus

❀

We have a little purse,
Made of ratching leather skin,
We want some of your small change,
To line it well within.

❀

Chorus

❀

Bring us out a table,
And spread it with a cloth,
Bring us out a cheese,
And of your Christmas loaf.

❀

Chorus

❀

God bless the master of this house,
Likewise the mistress, too,
And all the little children,
That round the table go.

❀

Chorus

We Three Kings of Orient Are

We three kings of Orient are,
Bearing gifts we traverse afar,
Field and fountain, moor and mountain,
Following yonder star.

Chorus:
O star of wonder, star of light,
Star with royal beauty bright,
Westward leading, still proceeding,
Guide us to thy perfect light.

Born a King on Bethlehem's plain,
Gold I bring to crown Him again,
King forever, ceasing never,
Over us all to reign.

Chorus

Frankincense to offer have I,
Incense owns a Deity nigh,

Prayer and praising, voices raising,
Worshipping God on high.

❀

Chorus

Myrrh is mine, its bitter perfume,
Breathes a life of gathering gloom,
Sorrowing, sighing, bleeding, dying,
Sealed in the stone cold tomb.

❀

Chorus

❀

Glorious now behold Him arise,
King and God and sacrifice,
Alleluia, Alleluia,
Sounds through the earth and skies.

❀

Chorus

We Wish You a
Merry Christmas

We wish you a Merry Christmas,
We wish you a Merry Christmas,
We wish you a Merry Christmas and,
A Happy New Year,
Good tidings we bring to you and your kin,
Good tidings for Christmas and a Happy New Year.

Oh, bring us a figgy pudding,
Oh, bring us a figgy pudding,
Oh, bring us a figgy pudding and a cup of good cheer,
We won't go until we get some,
We won't go until we get some,
We won't go until we get some,
So bring some right here.

We wish you a Merry Christmas,
We wish you a Merry Christmas,
We wish you a Merry Christmas and,
A Happy New Year.

What Child Is This?

What child is this who, laid to rest,
On Mary's lap is sleeping,
Whom Angels greet with anthems sweet,
While shepherds watch are keeping?

❦

This, this is Christ the King,
Whom shepherds guard and Angels sing,
Haste, haste, to bring Him laud,
The Babe, the Son of Mary.

❦

Why lies He in such mean estate,
Where ox and ass are feeding?
Good Christians, fear, for sinners here,
The silent Word is pleading.

❦

Nails, spear shall pierce Him through,
The cross be borne for me, for you,
Hail, hail the Word made flesh,
The Babe, the Son of Mary.

❦

So bring Him incense, gold and myrrh,
Come peasant, king to own Him,

The King of kings salvation brings,
Let loving hearts enthrone Him.

❀

Raise, raise a song on high,
The virgin sings her lullaby,
Joy, joy for Christ is born,
The Babe, the Son of Mary.

B.J. THOMAS
~ BIOGRAPHY ~

Billy Joe Thomas was born August 7th, 1942 at his grand-mother's home in Hugo, Oklahoma.

The family moved around often, but stayed in close proximity to Houston, Texas, during most of the children's growing years. The two Thomas boys both loved playing baseball and singing in their church choir.

Young Billy Joe adopted the nickname, B.J., when there were too many young men with the name of Billy Joe on his Little League Baseball team. The name followed him through life since that time.

During the past four decades, B.J. has:

- Sold more than 70 million records.

- Earned 2 Platinum records.

- Had 11 Gold records.

- Won 5 Grammy Awards.

- Won 2 Dove Awards for Gospel Recordings which include "Home Where I Belong."

- Had 15 Top 40 Pop/Rock Hits, which include "Raindrops Keep Fallin' On My Head," "Eyes Of A New York Woman," "Hooked On A Feeling," "Rock and Roll Lullaby," and "I Just Can't Help Believing."

- Had 10 Top 40 Country Chart Hits, which include "(Hey Won't You Play) Another Somebody Done Somebody Wrong Song," "Whatever Happened To Old Fashioned Love," and "Two Car Garage."

- Become the 60th Member of The Grand Ole Opry in 1981.

- Though no longer an active member of the Opry, B.J. still performs there as often as his schedule permits.

- Been the only artist ever to have the "Song Of The Year" on the Pop, Country and Gospel charts.

B.J. Thomas has been happily married for 39 years and is the father of 3 daughters.

∾ INDEX ∾